# The Pope's
# Greatest Adversary

*To Matt*

*My best friend and confidant, who has steadfastly put up with
me dragging him around Italy on research trips and cheered me on
when things have been tough.*

# The Pope's Greatest Adversary

## Girolamo Savonarola

Samantha Morris

PEN & SWORD HISTORY

First published in Great Britain in 2021 by
Pen & Sword History
An imprint of
Pen & Sword Books Ltd
Yorkshire – Philadelphia

ISBN 978 1 52672 444 1

A CIP catalogue record for this book is
available from the British Library.

Typeset by Mac Style
Printed and bound by CPI Group (UK) Ltd, Croydon, CR0 4YY

Pen & Sword Books Limited incorporates the imprints of Atlas,
Archaeology, Aviation, Discovery, Family History, Fiction, History,
Maritime, Military, Military Classics, Politics, Select, Transport,
True Crime, Air World, Frontline Publishing, Leo Cooper, Remember
When, Seaforth Publishing, The Praetorian Press, Wharncliffe
Local History, Wharncliffe Transport, Wharncliffe True Crime
and White Owl.

For a complete list of Pen & Sword titles please contact

PEN & SWORD BOOKS LIMITED
47 Church Street, Barnsley, South Yorkshire, S70 2AS, England
E-mail: enquiries@pen-and-sword.co.uk
Website: www.pen-and-sword.co.uk

Or

PEN AND SWORD BOOKS
1950 Lawrence Rd, Havertown, PA 19083, USA
E-mail: Uspen-and-sword@casematepublishers.com
Website: www.penandswordbooks.com

# Contents

# Acknowledgments

There are so many people that I would like to thank for their help and support in writing this book – too many in fact. The sheer amount of people that I owe gratitude to is long enough to be a book of its own, and honestly it has been so difficult to pick and choose who exactly to name here. But to each and every person who has been involved in this project even in the smallest way – thank you. You all mean the absolute world to me.

I would like to extend my heartfelt thanks to everyone at Pen and Sword for their tireless, professional and friendly attitude, not only towards my creating this book but to others past and in the pipeline for the future. Special thanks go to Jonathan Wright, my commissioning editor – without his belief in these projects, I would still be sitting there wondering if I was good enough to write anything. To the wonderful artists who have designed the cover for this project – thank you! Your beautiful work has added the final, perfect garnish to this book, and I couldn't be more grateful. To Rosie Crofts – your enthusiasm for history of all eras is a pleasure to see.

Special thanks go to the Medici Archive Project in Florence who have pointed me in the direction of various sources both secondary and printed primary, as well as the fantastic staff at various museums related to Savonarola in the city of Florence – particularly at the Convent of San Marco and the Palazzo Vecchio. The staff in these beautiful places are incredibly knowledgeable and friendly, and happy to answer any and all questions that are put to them.

To Dawn for her constant pushing me to carry on writing even when I believed I couldn't; Jo (BFFs for life); Hasan Niyazi – Renaissance myth-buster extraordinaire, may you rest in peace my friend; Poppi and Yazz, Tim and Claire Ridgway; Sammy; Craig; Dani; Andrea; Melanie and to all the extremely heavy metal bands that have been blasted into my ears during the writing of this project.

Of course very special thanks have to go to my mum and dad for believing in me when I first started out on the journey towards publication and for their constant love and support. And to my partner, Matt – he has put up with me constantly being lost in the life of Savonarola and his contemporaries. Not only that, but he has accompanied me on so many research holidays and has managed to find an appreciation for the Italian Renaissance. I couldn't have done this without you.

# Author's Note

This book originally started out as a brief introduction to Savonarola's life; however I came to the decision that he needed something more. This Dominican friar was witness to some of the biggest events in Renaissance history and, in fact, was the driving force behind many of them. The journey of reading about this man is one that sees an intertwining of religion and politics, so I have tried to keep the details as simple as possible. Of course, his story cannot be told without bringing in the complicated politics of the city of Florence and of Italy at the time. I have endeavoured to keep these details as straightforward as I possibly can while still telling the full story of Savonarola and the world in which he lived. There are, of course, studies out there relating to Savonarola, and there is a list of sources available at the back of this book. I would particularly recommend Donald Weinstein's *Savonarola: The Rise and Fall of a Renaissance Prophet* and *Savonarola and Florence: Prophecy and Patriotism in the Renaissance* as well as Lauro Martines' *Scourge and Fire* and Paul Strathern's *Death in Florence*. All these biographies are excellent academic sources that provide a highly detailed account of Savonarola's life, his own academic work, his sermons and the politics of the time. It is my hope that this work will be able to stand shoulder to shoulder with these books and help bring Girolamo Savonarola further into the public eye, to tell his story and bring it to a new audience.

My own interest in him was piqued when, for my sins, I was watching Showtime's *The Borgias* – many of my readers will already know my opinions regarding that television series – so I began to look further into him. The Dominican friar who had stood up against the Pope became a niggle, and then an earworm, and it just wouldn't go away until I started reading about his life. Eventually he became another firm Renaissance favourite of mine, second only to the Borgia family. My interest grew even stronger when my partner and I took a trip to Florence and spent a good few hours wandering the halls of San Marco, the monastery that had been his home for so many years; sitting in the cell that held him at the end of his life and standing in the spot where he was executed. It certainly made me feel closer to the man that divided Florence straight down the middle. Our visit to Ferrara only made me love him all the more – the city of his birth has the most beautiful statue of him in the piazza outside the castello, and you can even walk down a street named after him, which is also the street on which he was born. Many of the photographs in the middle of the book were taken by my partner and me on our trips to Florence and Ferrara, and it is my hope that they, along with the story told within these pages, will inspire people to visit these beautiful cities and continue to learn about such a fascinating era in Renaissance history.

I must be honest and say that there were times when I found writing this extremely difficult and wanted to give up. The majority of this has been written during a very difficult time for me and for the wider world. I was around halfway through the writing process when it was announced that the UK was going into lockdown thanks to the outbreak of Covid-19. This awful virus has swept the world and taken loved ones from so many. When lockdown was announced – as someone with a chronic illness it was better that I stay inside and self-isolate – I thought this would be the perfect time for me to crack on and get writing. While that was the case to start with, the anxiety and cabin fever from being stuck inside caught up with me and I just didn't want to write any more. It was only thanks to the support of my partner, friends and family that I pulled myself out of that rut and put my nose back to the grindstone. I have also been dealing with some health issues, in particular with my eyes – I've had vision problems potentially linked to my Type 1 diabetes – which has, of course, been a worry. This has meant that the writing process has been slower than I would have liked and has, at times, been a massive challenge. But I feel that dealing with these challenges has made me work harder, and the support I have received through it all has been top notch.

There may have been dark moments and there may have been struggles, but overall this book has been a pleasure to write. The period in which this book is set is dark for many reasons – the bonfire of the vanities being the main one – but it is a truly important period in the history of the Italian Renaissance, Florence and indeed the entire Christian world. The events of Girolamo Savonarola's life in Florence inspired political and religious change and would inspire Martin Luther in the Protestant Reformation of the early sixteenth century. Some might think that the subjects here will be dry and dull, but I can assure you that they are far from that. In fact, the events leading up to Savonarola's execution in 1498 would make an exciting television series (I'm available if any producers need help with that).

I hope, dear readers, that you will enjoy our journey through one of the most torrid periods in Italian history. I would say pull up a chair in the tavern while you do so, however our titular character – I'm not sure I could call him a protagonist, really – would certainly not approve. Instead, take a seat with a nice cup of tea and join us as we head back in time and explore the life of the Pope's greatest adversary, Girolamo Savonarola.

Samantha Morris
Southampton
August 2020

# Introduction

To the casual tourist, the small circular plaque on the ground in front of the Piazza della Signoria is just a bit of decoration; the Latin text upon it of no importance whatsoever. But while thousands of feet trample over this plaque each day, some know it as a spot of great importance in the history of Florence and the Italian Renaissance as a whole. For it was here, before the imposing palazzo, that Girolamo Savonarola was executed. The Florentines react to his name with a mixture of awe and intense dislike, very similar to the division that he created during his lifetime. But despite this the man is remembered and even commemorated by the people of Florence. On 23 May every year, a crowd gathers here and flowers are left upon the plaque. The Mayor of Florence then invokes the name of Savonarola before leading a procession to the Ponte Vecchio where the ceremony ends with flower petals being scattered on the water – just as Savonarola's remains had been scattered there so many centuries ago. This is an act of remembrance for a man who practically ruled the city from his pulpit. He was certainly no saint, and yet he fully believed in the message that he was sending out to the people of Florence – tyranny was unwelcome in the city and belief in God could 'make Florence great again'. Ironically, in his belief that tyranny was not welcome he became a tyrant himself, which the Florentine citizens simply could not tolerate. He may have done some good in getting rid of the dictatorial ruling Medici family, but, eventually, the Florentines decided that his puritanical rule was too much for them – they missed their gambling and sexual adventures.

The ceremony that takes place in the Piazza della Signoria each year is carried out so that people can remember Girolamo Savonarola and all that he stood for – whether he was a saint or sinner is unimportant. What matters is that he is a huge part of the history of Florence and he deserves to be remembered. But it was not always the case. In 1770, the ceremony was banned by the Florentine government – they did not want to pay homage to a man who had held Florence in his iron grip for so long and who had ousted the leading family from its place at the top of the social hierarchy. It is only recently, with a growing interest in the history – both good and bad – of the city, that the ceremony of remembrance has come back into play.

The word 'tyranny' is one that will pop up frequently within the story of Girolamo Savonarola. School textbooks a generation ago often referred to Italy as a geographical expression before 1861. It was in that year that Camillo Benso, Count Cavour and the red-shirted freedom fighter Giuseppe Garibaldi forged a single state from many in the Risorgimento which created modern Italy.

When the Roman empire fragmented in the fifth century in the wake of barbarian invasions, half of it split to form the Byzantine empire based at Constantinople. Italy itself collapsed into a number of minor states, ruled by a prince who was head of a particular family. It is tempting to see a forerunner of the mafia of the nineteenth/twentieth centuries in all this; how is the empire of Al Capone radically different from the Medicis or the Sforzas?

Central Italy was dominated by the papacy. While the extent of the current pope's power is limited in an administrative sense to the Vatican, the city within the city, in the late Middle Ages it covered all of Rome and the countryside to the north and south, the Romagna. The pope had always held a dual role. On the one hand he was God's vicar on earth, the papa, the father of his flock. On the other, he was an Italian princeling, deeply enmeshed in the often vicious politics of the day. Julius II, for example, the patron of Michelangelo of Sistine chapel ceiling fame, personally led his armies into battle, convincing himself and his followers that this was God's will.

To the south was the kingdom of the two Sicilies, the island of Sicily itself and the tip of Italy dominated by Naples. There was a French connection here which was highly relevant in Savonarola's time and dated back to another Norman conquest in the late eleventh century. It was in the north of Italy Savonarola's birthplace that complications arose. The norm for Medieval government throughout Europe was actually despotism, a duke, a king or emperor or overlord ran the area because he was rich and had castles and troops to see that his bidding was carried out. In two north Italian cities in particular, Savonarola's Florence and nearby Venice, they were governed in the form of elected councils. This was a pale imitation of ancient Roman history and a living example of the schizoid regime of the time. Ancient Rome was originally governed, as all states were, by a king, a strong man who evoked all kinds of godly support to create a mystique of majesty. By the fifth century BC, however, the kings of Rome were regarded as cruel tyrants and their last ruler, Tarquinus Superbus (the great Tarquin) was overthrown.

In his place, the Romans set up a republic, in reality a series of committees spearheaded by the senate, that covered every aspect of government from war and foreign trade to water supplies and entertainment – the bread and circuses that the Romans loved. It is noticeable however that social hierarchies never actually disappeared. Unlike the modern United States that hijacked the name and concept of the senate, pre-Christian Rome was not remotely a democracy, nor did it pretend to be. The ruling elite who dominated the senate were the patricians, the rich landowning families, who lorded it over the plebians (everybody else). By the time of Christ, republican virtues were being challenged by what was, in effect, a return to kingship. Perhaps this was the natural order of things. Julius Caesar may have had ambitions in this respect, but his enemies killed him before he had the chance to grab the laurel wreath symbol. It was his adopted nephew Octavius who became Rome's first emperor as Augustus.

The situation in northern Italy by Savonarola's time had echoes of all this. The republican councils of Florence and Venice harked back to the senate tradition but the Medicis in Florence and the Doge in Venice were a reminder of the age of kings. It was not an easy alliance but it worked tolerably well unless a spanner was thrown into the works. That spanner was Girolamo Savonarola.

When he first arrived in the city of Florence in 1482, the city was under the rule of the Medici family – Lorenzo the Magnificent was at the top of both the social and political hierarchy, running the city as its de facto leader and prince. Of course, many people disliked the fact that the Medici family held such power, and many plots were conceived in an effort to topple its members. When Savonarola arrived, he would have already been acutely aware of the discontent the Medici family aroused in people and the assassination attempt that had been aimed at Lorenzo and his brother Giuliano. It had been big news in Florence – on 26 April 1478, as the Host (the consecrated body of Christ) was raised within a crowded Santa Maria del Fiore, carnage erupted. This moment was to be the finale of a conspiracy that had been instigated by the Pazzi family and its allies, in which the aim was to assassinate both Medici brothers. The Pazzis were consumed with jealousy – the Medici had climbed the social scale thanks to shrewd political machinations, while the position of the Pazzi had remained ineffective. Lorenzo de' Medici had power that many believed would be dangerous for the future of the republic. They saw him as a tyrant and he and his family became the target of resentment. There were those who took this a step further, believing that Lorenzo and Giuliano had to die in order to restore peace and stability. Unfortunately for the Pazzi, the plan to commit the double murder at Mass failed and while Giuliano was viciously murdered, Lorenzo managed to escape. His revenge on those who killed his brother and attempted to oust him from power was brutal. Those involved were hanged from the windows of the Piazza della Signoria or held as prisoners. Jacopo de' Pazzi had fled the city after the event, but was caught and hanged next to the corpses of his fellow conspirators.

Amidst the tumultuous political scene that was the Florentine government, Girolamo Savonarola would take the city by storm. The people flocked to his sermons, at first held within the monastery of San Marco and then later in the huge Cathedral of Santa Maria del Fiore. His words would be taken as prophecies, and his promises to the people had them hooked almost from the beginning. Savonarola's excellent oratory convinced the Florentines that he could change the city from a vice-loving Hell into a City of God. It was a dangerous hand for the friar to play as, despite having the love of the ordinary people, he would end up making enemies of some of the most dangerous men in the Catholic Church – including Pope Alexander VI. This would lead to his downfall and to the people who loved him turning on him completely. It was a pattern in Florence that would be repeated time and again; the citizens would turn on the Medici – even leading to the family's expulsion from the city in 1494 – and they would turn on their beloved friar once they realised he could not, and did not, speak for God as he believed so ardently.

The city of Florence during this time was the centre of a republic that included the territories of Pisa, Lucca and Arezzo. Rather than being ruled by a single prince, as most of the Italian states were, Florence was ruled by its people and an elected government. To prevent any one man from gaining too much power, many individuals only held offices for a matter of months before being replaced. However, the ballots were often rigged so that with each change of government there was always a pro-Medici majority within the administration, which was known as the Signoria. And beneath the façade of a freely elected government, the Medici took on the roles of unofficial rulers. They were the heads of state who were also the unelected princes of the republic. Girolamo Savonarola saw this, disliked it, and became the catalyst for great change within the city.

This is the story of a man who climbed his way to the very top. This is the story of a man who took the city by storm thanks to his belief in God and that the corruption of the Church needed to be dealt with. He believed so wholeheartedly in the message he was giving that he gave his life for it. It is the story of a man who held an entire city under his spell. Girolamo Savonarola's life is a fascinating insight into the mind of a religious fanatic; a man who hooked the citizens of Florence with his powerful rhetoric and promises of reformation. This book aims to tell his story from beginning to end, with all the twists and political turns in between. It aims to bring his story to those new to the subject of the Italian Renaissance and tell it in a manner that works for everyone, whether new to the subject or not.

We start, therefore, with his birth and early life. It is the beginning of a path that would eventually lead him to joining Holy Orders that would end in horrific torture and brutal execution.

# Chapter 1

# On the Ruin of the World

On 21 September 1452, screams could be heard coming from behind the walls of a little house on what is now known as the Via Savonarola in Ferrara, as Elena Bonacossi, wife of Niccolò Savonarola, gave birth to a baby boy. No one present at the birth could have imagined that this tiny little thing would cause such a stir in his later years. The child was named Girolamo and he spent his childhood in the bustling city of Ferrara.

Ferrara itself was rich and has been described by many as the first modern city in the Western world. It was a city that encouraged music, art and study, and it exuded luxury: the higher classes were envied for their sumptuous clothes and adornments, while those lower down the social scale never went hungry – unlike many rulers, those who governed Ferrara made sure that there was always a stockpile of flour in case of bad harvests.

At the time of Savonarola's birth, Ferrara was the capital of a large state in the north of Italy and was governed by the powerful Este family, whose court was one of the finest in the country. The city's skyline was dominated by the huge structure of the Castello Estense, only a stone's throw away from the Basilica of San Giorgio. The castle towered over the town and even today, it is an imposing sight. During the reign of the Este, however, it must have served as a dramatic reminder of the family's power. The castle was not where the Este had their main court – they lived and entertained at the Palazzo del Corte, just a short walk away, which now houses the municipal offices of the commune of Ferrara. The castello was only used by members of the Este family in times of extreme danger, until the fifteenth century, when they moved their court permanently inside its walls.

The castello was built in 1385, after the citizens of Ferrara rose up against the Estensi family. They were angered by the fact that they were on the edge of ruin after being taxed to high heaven, and flooding had seriously affected their livelihoods. In fury, they tore apart Tommaso da Tortona, the man who was responsible for resolving the situation – something which he had clearly failed to do. This incident convinced the Marquis of Ferrara that his home was unsafe and not suitable for any sort of protection, so he ordered a castle to be built, incorporating the Torre del Leoni with a passageway connecting the new fortress to the palace. This extensive new fortress was also used to house prisoners, with dank, damp and claustrophobic dungeons being constructed in the lower levels. Pasquale Villari, Savonarola's first biographer, recounts the contrast between the opulence of the upper storeys and the awful sounds that came from those kept below:

> In those times no one thought of visiting for amusement the subterranean dungeons guarded by seven gratings from the light of day. They were full of immured victims and the clanking of chains and groans of human beings in pain could be heard from their depths, mingling with the strains of music and ceaseless revelry going on above, the ringing of silver plate, the clatter of majolica dishes and the clinking of venetian glass.[1]

It would not have been a secret to the nobles who gathered in the Este court that there were prisoners kept below them, though they were unlikely to ever have set foot in a dungeon themselves. Today, tourists are able to visit these cells and cannot help but feel a sense of profound unease that swells as they duck through the doorways. These cold and damp cells, with their tiny windows, may be brightly lit today, but it is easy to imagine being locked away in one of these dank little rooms. How many went mad down there? How many men and women lost their lives while kept prisoner in these cells? One well-known inmate was Giulio d'Este, the brother of Alfonso I, who, in 1506, organised a plot to eliminate Alfonso and another brother, Ippolito (who had beaten Giulio to such an extent the year before that he had damaged his eyesight permanently), and place his other brother, Ferrante, at the head of the family. It did not succeed and both brothers were locked in the dungeons beneath the castle. Ferrante died while incarcerated, but Giulio was eventually freed at the age of 81, after fifty-three years in prison.

The Este family were great patrons of music, art and study and, in 1442, Leonello d'Este reopened Ferrara's university, which had been founded by his grandfather. This was to be a shining light in Ferrara and established itself as a centre of great learning; teaching a mixture of Humanism (which put Man, rather than God, at the centre of all things and, in a way, was the end of Medieval civilization and heralded a new world of natural law and science), mathematics and astrology. Leonello also established a department of medicine, specifically for Michele Savonarola, an academic from Padua who had recently settled in Ferrara; it was Michele who would be a big part of young Girolamo, his grandson's, upbringing.

Born in 1385, Michele was of Paduan descent, and settled in Ferrara in 1440 where he began a successful career teaching at the university. It was there that he caught the eye of the Este rulers and was offered the post of physician to the court. He was so successful, and thought of so highly, that Pope Nicholas made him a Knight of St John of Jerusalem, a high honour within the Church. These knights were more commonly known as the Knights Hospitaller and their mission, from their creation in the twelfth century, was originally to care for sick and injured pilgrims visiting the Holy Land. Later they were charged with the defence of the kingdom of Jerusalem and turned into a military order. It became associated with physicians, and even today exists as the St. John's Ambulance Brigade, a team of volunteers who both deliver and train in first aid and offer first emergency response support in many life-threatening situations.

Michele remained as physician in the Este court through the reigns of later rulers – Leonello d'Este even increased his salary and exempted him from all duties, other than his medical work, to allow him time to spend time on what would become some of the most pioneering texts of the age. Not only did he complete *Practica Medicinae Sive De Aegritudinibus* (*The*

*Practice of Medicine from Head to Toe)*, his other works include *Practica Maior* (*Greater Practice*), *Speculum Phisionomie* (*Speculum Physiognomy*) and *De nuptiis Batibecho et Seraboca* (*The Marriage of Batibecho and Seraboca*). He was also one of the first people to note that if plague victims were kept in quarantine it helped to stop the spread of the disease. Those who were already isolated were less likely to contract it. 'Why does it commonly happen that in a town in which inhabitants are dying of plague, some people who are locked up, like monks or prisoners, remain untouched?' he queried.[2]

Groundbreaking at the time, it was, however, explained away with old-fashioned medieval viewpoints. There was no science to explain that the idea of distancing and quarantine helped stop the spread of diseases such as the plague – instead it was put forward that thicker air in enclosed spaces meant the disease found it more difficult to spread, and that prisoners, for instance, ate a lot of garlic which purified the air. Still, the question that Michele Savonarola asked was one that began the long journey into the cure of infectious diseases.

Not much is known about Girolamo's childhood, but we do know that he was a very intelligent young man, highly strung and fond of his family. According to a contemporary biographer, Michele's tutelage resulted in: 'Reaching the age for learning manners and letters, his grandfather still being alive, he made no small progress at grammar and Latin.'[3]

As well as Latin, it is likely that he would have learned Greek and Hebrew. Michele also taught his grandson about Thomas Aquinas, a thirteenth-century Dominican friar and theologian whose work became a core programme of study for those wishing to enter the Church. Many of Aquinas' ideas became hugely influential to philosophers and theologians in the centuries after his death. Even today he is believed to be one of the greatest philosophers in Church history, and his work is still used in the teaching of new members of the priesthood in the Catholic Church. In a nutshell, Aquinas' central thesis was that reason is found in God, and that man has the natural capacity for knowledge without the need for any form of divine revelation. However, divine revelation can give mankind extra knowledge – and he makes the point that other things can go through a change with something else added to them. Water, for instance, can heat with its own form of divine revelation – that is to say by placing it over a fire. There is much more to Aquinas' philosophy than that, and so much information that it would warrant a book of its own. Savonarola developed a lifelong adoration of the philosopher thanks to his grandfather's lessons. Michele did not believe in the new-fangled Humanism that had swept its way through Europe – although it must be noted that throughout the fifteenth century, the study of Aquinas remained popular amongst the Humanists of the age; his work bridging the gap between the old world inhabited by Michele Savonarola and their new approach.

The young Girolamo would have gone to lectures at the university in Ferrara where he 'attended the school of the poets', which meant he studied the works of classical authors such as Plato and Socrates. This inspired him to begin writing poetry in the same form as Petrarch, a poet and scholar who lived in the early fourteenth century. Later he would state that God turned him away from the study of these Humanist poets and scholars, tearing up all the work he had ever written about them.[4]

On 17 May 1459, Ferrara had the honour of hosting a visit by Pius II. He was making his way throughout Italy in order to convince his flock that they should join him on a crusade to take Constantinople back from the Turks. Six years earlier, the capital of Byzantium, the eastern part of the Roman empire, had been destroyed by the Ottoman Turks under their Sultan, Mehmet II. Christendom was outraged. The great church of Hagia Sofia had become a mosque and a way of life that had lasted for eleven hundred years, had come to an abrupt end. It was during this visit to Ferrara that the young Savonarola would have had his first look at Rodrigo Borgia. At this point, Borgia was a young cardinal who had risen through the ranks thanks to his uncle, Pope Callixtus III. He was generally well liked and often caught the eye of the ladies – throughout his ecclesiastical career he was known to keep a multitude of mistresses, including Vannozza Cattanei who would become the mother of his most famous and notorious children. Borgia was a clever man with an astute political mind. It was thanks to his unscrupulous scheming in the most recent conclave that Pius was elected. The Pope remained grateful to Borgia throughout his life, despite disagreeing with much of the cardinal's behaviour. When Pius died in 1464, Borgia backed Pietro Barbo, who became Paul II upon his accession to the throne of St Peter. Paul was the archetypical Renaissance pope, keeping a mistress and not being secretive about it – although many popes before him had done exactly the same thing. Borgia, who had been vice chancellor since his uncle's reign, remained in the post and bided his time, waiting for the perfect moment to strike and become pope himself.

The Este court, like nearly every ducal and royal court in Europe, was full of pomp and ostentation. Borso d'Este, who had taken over after the death of Leonello, was known for his love of vice. Yet he did not take a mistress – no contemporary chronicler makes mention of him ever contemplating taking a wife, but they do write about him spending rather a lot of time with close male friends. Many now take this as an indication that Borso was homosexual and any rumours of such goings on would have completely shocked the people of Ferrara. After all, sodomy was a sin punishable by death. The amount of money that Borso spent on his court and, in particular, himself was mind boggling. Examples of his squandering include buying the dukedom of Ferrara for himself from the Holy Roman Emperor, Frederick III, thus moving from being a simple marquis to a duke, and sending a statue of himself to Florence. He certainly thought highly of himself, but Michele disliked his attitude and the way he wasted his wealth. Girolamo would inherit his grandfather's sense of disdain and disapproval of such behaviour. In fact, the young boy was taken to court just once and was so disgusted by what he saw that he refused ever to set foot in those buildings again.

Michele Savonarola died in 1468, aged 83, leaving his son Niccolò as patriarch of the family. He could not have been any more different from his father; although trained in banking, that career had failed miserably when he underwrote loans without any form of security. He also loitered around the Este court and managed to make friends with people who had very expensive tastes, throwing the money left by his father and his wife's dowry down the drain. It was Niccolò who convinced his son to study for his Master of Arts in medicine simply for his own selfish ends. He wanted Girolamo to earn enough money to pay off the huge debts he had racked up with his inability to control his finances. Yet the home he shared with his wife Elena, and the upbringing they gave their children, was affectionate, and the family was very close. So when Girolamo eventually made the decision to leave Ferrara – and the potentially lucrative world of medicine – to join the Dominican Order without a word to his parents, the news was taken badly.

To start with, Girolamo was happy enough to follow in his grandfather's footsteps and recall Michele's tuition, but then he began learning, and indeed leaning, towards the more fashionable themes of Humanism – something that would have his grandfather turning in his grave. At one point the quiet young man – not yet the splendid orator he would become – began to write poetry and play the lute. A neighbour of the family caught his eye and he fell in love. The girl in question was named Laudomia, an illegitimate member of the distinguished Strozzi family who had taken refuge in Ferrara from Florence. They got to know one another by leaning out of the upper-storey windows and talking across the narrow alleyway between their two houses. The lovestruck young man even tried to serenade her with his lute playing. But Laudomia rejected his advances and broke his heart when she refused his offer of marriage, stating that no Strozzi would ever marry into a family as low born as the Savonarolas. He spat back that no Savonarola would ever marry a bastard.[5] His brother Mauro recounted this to one of Girolamo's first biographers; apparently from that moment on, Girolamo resolved to 'shun the world and all its vanities'.[6]

He appeared to sink into an almost depressive state following his rejection. He developed a hatred of the corruption within the Church, along with a growing dislike of how those in power squandered their wealth. Savonarola had watched as Ferrara had been thrown into a brutal civil war following the death of Borso, the outcome of which had seen Ercole d'Este taking over as Duke and Niccolò d'Este, the other claimant to the title, being beheaded. As well as this, the new Pope, Sixtus IV, was guilty of some colossal extravagance. Savonarola began to write poems about how the Church was falling into ruin and how he was surrounded by vice. He called Rome the 'whore of Babylon'. One poem, entitled *On the Ruin of the World*, criticises the Church and the ostentation of the rich:

> My song, take care not to put your trust in the colour purple
> Flee palaces and balconies
> And take care to share your thoughts with few
> So that to the whole world you will be hostile.[7]

It was these fervent beliefs, along with a visit to Faenza in 1474, that convinced him to enter the Church and give up all plans of becoming a physician.

He arrived during the celebrations for May Day, which drove him to seek shelter inside the Church of Sant Agostino. As he stepped inside, a friar was delivering the daily sermon, the text of which was taken from the book of Genesis, where God spoke to Abraham telling him to: 'Go forth out of thy country, and from thy kindred, and out of thy father's house, and come into the land that I shall show thee.'[8]

To Savonarola, in that moment, God was speaking directly to him through the voice of the preaching friar. He knew that it was his purpose, his destiny, to abandon his family, give up everything he had in the world and take Holy Orders.

It took him a year to carry this out, as he had no wish to have his mother become hysterical at the thought of his leaving. He knew it would be best for him to slip away in secret, so he had to wait for the right moment. That opportunity came on 23 April 1475, when Ferrara was celebrating St George's Day. It was a huge festival that included events such as the Palio horse race, boating on the river and a crossbow competition in the main piazza. While his parents were enjoying the festivities, Girolamo Savonarola left his home and city of his birth and walked thirty miles to Bologna, where he entered a Dominican friary and told them that he wished to join their Order.

The next day, he wrote a letter to his family in an effort to explain why he had disappeared without so much as a goodbye. He wrote:

> I should like you to know, however, that I was in such a terrible state that if I had revealed just how much I was suffering at the prospect of leaving you, I think my heart would have broken and that I could

not have gone on with it … [I can] no longer bear the wickedness of the people of Italy … . Put an end to your weeping and spare me any further sadness and pain than I suffer already.[9]

Is it any wonder that the letter was not received well by his parents? One can only imagine their reaction when they read his words. A month or so later he wrote a sterner second letter to them, evidently having run out of patience with their unhappiness over his decision:

What are you crying about, you blind ones? Why so much weeping and grumbling, people without light? If our prince (of Ferrara), reaching out among the people, had asked me to strap on a sword and become one of his knights, to what jubilation and feasting you would have treated yourselves! And if I had rejected the request which of you would not have thought me crazy? Oh you without common sense, oh blind fools and without a ray of faith! The Prince of princes, he who is infinite power calls me with a loud voice.[10]

He tempered his ire in the closing lines, telling his family that they should be happy that he has chosen to be a 'doctor of souls, rather than a doctor of the body'.

This young Dominican novitiate had started on a path to what would be a remarkable life. Did he have any idea just how much of an exalted position he would end up enjoying? It seems not, but what is clear is that Girolamo Savonarola had begun a journey that would bring him face to face with some of the most powerful people in Renaissance Italy.

# Chapter 2

# The Young Dominican

What was it that inspired Savonarola to join the Dominican Order? Founded by Dominic Guzman in 1203, the simple Order consisted of travelling preachers who lived plain lives – charity was the order of the day and they owned nothing except the shabby robes on their backs and a few books. They were intelligent men and when he began the Order, Dominic had insisted that each priory had a teacher who would train its new recruits in the basics before packing them off to university to study theology. Many of the high-ranking members of the Order also taught at the universities.

The Dominican Order was known to have housed many of the greatest minds in history, including Thomas Aquinas. Yet from the moment he arrived in Bologna, Savonarola spent his time locked away. He would go for days without food and slept beneath a sack, refusing to study and arguing that while the Dominicans had previously hosted excellence, he himself did not want to become an 'Aristotle in the Cloister'.[1] He spent a year as a novitiate before taking his vows to become a fully fledged friar and it was only then that he went back to his studies. It was insisted upon – mainly because it was seen as an outstanding centre of learning – that he went back to the books. Under the tutelage of Frate (Fra) Pietro da Bergamo, he began to study theology and made such quick progress that within three years he was appointed as an assistant lecturer on the subject. He stated later that his first year in the friary had been the happiest of his life as he had found a form of freedom in being told what to do, and when to do it. A life of self-denial and complete abstinence was certainly welcomed by the young novitiate.

Despite wishing to escape his family in Ferrara, Savonarola initially found himself with some misgivings on entering the Order. He believed, he later told his biographer, that the simple life he yearned for could not be found in the monastery. He was also afraid of just how learned the Dominican Order was when it came to the study of Aristotelian philosophy and science – he had, after all, grown up with that sort of tutelage thanks to his grandfather, and he was afraid that his Dominican brothers would force him into studying more of it. All he wanted was a simple life, not one of more learning. He would have been happy performing menial tasks such as gardening or sewing[2], but soon found himself settled into the monastic life. His fears, it seemed, were completely ungrounded.

He was content in the friary and his mood began to shift from the depressed young man who hated the world to one that was much more positive. He still harboured the belief that much of the Church was corrupt, but he found hope in his new life a happiness that he had never known before.

Savonarola finished his novitiate a year later and took his vows. At this point he was required to continue his studies and begin to learn the art of preaching. After all, the Dominicans were an order of preachers and the young friar was not yet a distinguished speaker. Aware he lacked public-speaking ability, he sought advice from some eminent Humanists in Rome – advice that he ultimately rejected. Perhaps, had he listened, he would have found his voice much earlier than he did.

Four years after entering the friary at Bologna, Savonarola found himself back in his hometown. He had been sent there to teach the young novices of the Dominican friary. Yet he saw little of the family that he had left behind – they had fallen on hard times and had been forced to sell their home to their neighbours, the Strozzi. He did not seem unduly bothered by that, spending his time teaching new friars and starting his journey into preaching. At this stage in his career, his efforts were disappointing. It would take a long time before he became the confident orator that would pack out churches in Florence. But despite his failures, which he would later recount in a letter to his mother, his superiors within the friary still sent him to preach in cities across the north of Italy.

Politics at this time was turbulent, particularly in the city that would become Savonarola's home – Florence. In 1478, a huge scandal would grip the city. Known as the Pazzi conspiracy, a group of men tried to assassinate Lorenzo de' Medici, the leader of Florence in all but name. This was a move that had been backed by the Pope at the time, Sixtus. Event began in 1476 with the assassination of Lorenzo's ally, the Duke of Milan, Galeazzo Maria Sforza, by three men while on the way to Mass in the Duomo. It was 26 December, and as the duke prepared to make his way to the cathedral, his wife, Bona of Savoy, begged him not to go as the weather was horrendous, but Sforza argued that the choir, of which he was so proud, had already gone ahead. So off he rode – it would be the last time his wife or children ever saw him. Once he reached the cathedral, he dismounted and entered the beautiful building surrounded by lackeys and petitioners. As he made his way down the nave towards his seat, he was approached by a man who often made petitions to him. But this time things were different. As Andrea Lampugnano knelt and swept his cap from his head, assassins burst through the crowd. It was Lampugnano who got in the first hit, stabbing Sforza in the chest. He was then surrounded and stabbed over and over again. His last words as he fell to the cold marble floor were, 'I am dead.'[3]

Sforza's heir was a 7-year-old boy, so Milan was thrown into complete and utter chaos. It also meant that Florence would not be able to rely on their ally should something awful come to pass, so it was the perfect opportunity for those who had grown tired of Medici rule to strike. In 1477, the main conspirators, Girolamo Riario, Archbishop of Pisa, Francesco Salviati and Francesco de' Pazzi, met in Rome where they agreed to kill the head of the Medici family, as well as his brother, Giuliano.[4] The death of the brothers would clear the way for the Pazzi family to step up to where they believed they should be – rulers of Florence, and head of the biggest banking business in the city. They had, after all, already taken over the papal accounts, which was a massive blow to the Medici business and, ultimately, its wealth. The plot even had the backing of Pope Sixtus who, although repeatedly telling the conspirators (one of whom, Riario, was his nephew) that he would not condone killing, made sure to tell them in the end, 'Go and do what you will.'[5]

It was agreed that the deed would be done during Mass at the Cathedral of Santa Maria del Fiore on Sunday, 26 April 1478, and that once the city had been freed from Medici tyranny they would all go to the palace and share in a huge banquet.

That morning, the conspirators found out that Giuliano was not planning on attending Mass as usual. He had been suffering terribly with a bad leg and wished to stay at home resting. Concerned that the plan would fall at the first hurdle, de' Pazzi and Salviati hurried back to the Medici palace to convince him to go. He agreed, and as they made their way down the Via Larga towards the cathedral, Pazzi threw an arm around his old friend. Yet this was not a friendly gesture. Rather, it was in order to check if the youngest Medici was wearing armour beneath his clothing. He was not.

The signal for the murders was the raising of the Host during High Mass. Afterwards, witnesses claim that the first blow hit Giuliano when Bernardo Baroncelli cried out 'Here traitor!' and stabbed him in the chest.[6] As the injured man staggered backwards, he was struck by a second assailant – his so-called friend Francesco de' Pazzi – who got himself into such a frenzy that he managed to stab his own thigh. Giuliano's body was covered in nineteen stab wounds and he was left for dead on the floor of the cathedral.[7] Meanwhile Lorenzo, unaware of his brother's fate, was dealing with his own attackers; two priests had settled themselves behind him and when the signal came, had thrust their hidden daggers forward. Yet one of them made the mistake of grabbing Lorenzo's shoulder, probably in order to steady himself, or perhaps in an effort to turn his victim around, and it alerted Lorenzo to what was happening. Instead of receiving a dagger in the chest, he managed to escape with a small wound in his neck thanks to the way he lurched forward. As he did so, he hoisted his mantle over his arm and shoulder in order to use it as a shield. He pulled his short sword free before jumping over the wooden rail that surrounded the octagonal choir area and quickly made for the safety of the north sacristy. Francesco Nori, a friend and employee of Lorenzo's, pulled his master to safety and was mortally wounded for his efforts. Lorenzo and a number of his friends were able to get themselves safely into the sacristy where the huge bronze doors were locked – guides still gleefully point out these doors on tours of the cathedral. As the men waited for the chaos to die down, they began to worry that Lorenzo's wound had been infected with poison and Antonio Ridolfi made the brave decision to suck at the wound and remove any potential deadly threats to Lorenzo's life. All the while Lorenzo was asking desperately if anyone had seen his brother, but no one knew of Giuliano's fate.[8]

At some point – whether it was minutes or hours later is unknown – there came a pounding upon the huge bronze doors. Who could it be? Friend or foe? Sigismondo della Stufa, a dear friend of Lorenzo's, took himself up into the organ gallery to see who was causing such a commotion and there he saw the frantic faces of friends and family who were desperate to know if Lorenzo de' Medici had survived.

The doors were opened, and Lorenzo and his entourage made their way back to the Medici palace on the Via Larga. While Lorenzo did not catch a glimpse of his brother's mangled body on the floor, Angelo Poliziano, a close friend of both the brothers, did. He was so horrified, he could not bear to cover the body of his good friend and instead hurried away. It was only later that day that Lorenzo would learn that his brother had died.

While all of this was going on, another part of the conspiracy was taking place just across the city. The Archbishop of Pisa, Francesco Salviati, and a number of retainers moved on to the Palazzo della Signoria (today known as the Palazzo Vecchio) where they were let in without any problems. As the archbishop went upstairs to see the head of government, some of his crowd remained on the lower floor where they intended to overpower any guards they might find. The excuse given for the archbishop's visit to the gonfalonier (captain general), Cesare Petrucci, was that he had a message from the Pope for him. The two went into a private meeting where the Florentine churchman spun an intricate yarn that His Holiness was planning on honouring Petrucci's son in Rome. Yet he began to stumble over his words, immediately alerting the gonfalonier that something was amiss, and he called for the guards. The archbishop made a run for it with Petrucci hot on his tail, but he was surprised to see Jacopo Bracciolini, the local writer, famous classicist and hanger-on of Archbishop Salviati, who was so wildly out of place within the government building that it was becoming clearer by the second that something was very wrong; more so when Bracciolini drew a weapon. Petrucci was obviously alert that day, as he grabbed the man by his hair, threw him to the ground and ordered one of the guards to take him prisoner. No one would come to help the archbishop now – the rest of his followers had been trapped in the warren of rooms on the lower floors of the palace.

The alarm was raised. At around midday the great bell (*vacca*) was tolled and word began to spread that someone had tried to murder the Medici brothers. Other rumours claimed both had been killed. It would take a while for the outcome of the day's bloody events to become clear.

As Jacopo de' Pazzi marched on the Piazza della Signoria, shouting for liberty and freedom from the Medici tyranny, the people, having got wind of the plot to overthrow their leader, turned on the conspirators. Archbishop Salviati was flung from a window of the palazzo still dressed in his vestments, to dangle at the end of a rope. Shortly after, Lorenzo quashed rumours of his death by appearing on the balcony of his palazzo to address the crowd, the increasingly bloodthirsty people of Florence. His speech made one thing clear – he would be taking revenge on anyone who had a hand in murdering his brother and the attempted coup.

That revenge came swiftly. Lorenzo ordered that members of the Pazzi family were killed, imprisoned or banished from Florence. Their wealth and property were seized, and their name was all but wiped from the city. When he found out exactly who was involved, he began hunting down those directly implicated in the plot against him. The conspirators were quickly caught. Francesco de' Pazzi, who had wounded himself in his frenzied stabbing of Giuliano, was found hiding in the family home and dragged to the Palazzo della Signoria where he was stripped naked and hanged from one of the windows. The same fate awaited Jacopo de' Pazzi. He had been loath to take part having seen how weak the plan was, but had been talked into it and had tried to escape – as had Antonio Maffei, who had been one of the two priests (the other being Stefano da Bagnone) to attack Lorenzo.[9] They had stepped in after military leader Giovanni Battista da Montesecco, who had been commissioned personally to take part in the assassination, refused saying he 'could not bring himself to kill a man in a place where "God would see him.""[10]

Pope Sixtus reacted quickly, seizing all the Medici assets in Rome, and excommunicating Lorenzo and the entire government of Florence. However, Lorenzo ignored this and the citizens supported the Medici, refusing to rise up and join the conspirators. To the majority of Florentines, the Medici were their leaders and they would never rise in support of a few disgruntled noblemen.

How would Savonarola have felt in regard to these events? He already had strong viewpoints on the corruption of the ducal courts thanks to his childhood in Ferrara, but hearing how the Medici had executed an archbishop must have caused him great unease. And one can only imagine his horror when he heard how Lorenzo had decided to ignore the excommunication or interdict on Florence by the Pope. The young churchman must have felt some form of sympathy for the conspirators. This awful moment in the history of Florence would certainly help him form opinions that would ultimately shape his involvement in the politics of that same city.

When the war of Ferrara broke out in 1482, the University was closed which meant that Savonarola would have to leave the city. The conflict had started as a petty dispute between Duke Ercole d'Este and Venice over salt dues – the Pope decided to back Venice as he wanted to oust Ercole from his place and install his nephew instead. Pope Sixtus offered the Venetians Reggio and Modena if they took Ferrara in his name and when they agreed, he sent papal troops to help them in their efforts. Ferrara was only saved when the Neapolitan army arrived to help Ercole. When Pope Sixtus realised that Venice actually wanted to take the whole duchy for themselves, he swiftly changed sides! The war raged on for two years and Savonarola's superiors ordered him to leave the city – which thankfully was not completely destroyed – and take up a post in Florence, as a senior lecturer in the Convent of San Marco.

Located within the heart of Florence and not far from the imposing Cathedral of Santa Maria del Fiore, San Marco had been founded in 1299, but was so neglected by the Sylvestrine Order who lived there that, in 1436, Pope Eugenius IV gave the convent to the Dominican Order. The complex had been entirely rebuilt and renovated by the renowned architect Michelozzo Michelozzi and the project had been funded by Cosimo de' Medici, patriarch of the family at the time. He also provided the friars with a number of items for use in their daily lives, including vestments, services and books from his own vast library. Cosimo even had his own cell within the convent decorated with beautiful frescoes painted by Fra Angelico, a Dominican brother. Not only did he decorate the cell of the convent's patron, but the cells of his brothers were also painted with scenes depicting the life of Christ.[11] The Dominicans had a rule that cells could only be decorated with images of the Virgin Mary, the crucifixion and the life of St Dominic but Angelico bent these rules and included far more in Christ's life than his crucifixion. The Cloister of St Antonino is decorated with more of Angelico's beautiful frescoes, while the great refectory holds a later fresco by the artist Giovanni Antonio Sogliani. The chapter house contains a large fresco by Angelico entitled *Crucifixion with Saints*, while the small refectory on the ground floor is dominated by Domenico Ghirlandaio's *Last Supper*.[12] These frescoes were there to show the glory of God, not only to the brothers but also to visitors.

Almost immediately, Savonarola proved himself to be a successful lecturer and a popular member of the convent. It was, in particular, his hard line when it came to observing the Dominican vows of poverty that made his fellow brothers sit up and take notice. They may have lived within the walls of a particularly lavish monastical complex, but the monks obviously felt some sort of affinity with the senior lecturer and his moral stance. And his popularity grew so much that after just two short months he was made Novice Master of San Marco.

Savonarola not only taught the young novices, he also produced a number of textbooks during these early years; the books were basic school guides which introduced the ideas of Aristotle and logic. Yet already the young monk was beginning to grow uncomfortable in the city he now called home. From within the safety of the monastery walls, he would have been able to observe how lawless the city had become and the increasingly Humanist leanings of the nobility, scholars and even other men of the Church. One particular friar who managed to enrage Savonarola was Fra Mariano who was known to quote ancient works from Greece and Rome in his sermons rather than the Bible. This was abhorrent to the novice master who decided that it was time he started preaching himself. He would make sure that the word of God reached the people not only of Florence, but the whole of Italy, and stop the spread of the disease of Humanism. But there was a problem – he had no confidence in his abilities as an orator and was unable to raise his voice to such a level that it would inspire fear in a gathered congregation. Later, in a letter to his mother, he would admit that his early sermons could 'not move a hen'.[13]

His first sermons were given to his brothers within the walls of San Marco and he soon moved to the Monastero delle Murate, where he preached to the Benedictine nuns who lived there. He made notes following each sermon, commenting on the reaction of his audiences, and he often criticised his own work.

The lack of a congregation was a major sticking point for Savonarola. There were times when he would preach to fewer than twenty-five people, the majority of whom were children who had been brought to church by their parents; and those who did show up were almost instantly put off by his strong Ferrarese accent. People were rather bored with the scholastic preaching that the Dominicans had been practising for centuries. Even Savonarola found the old methods dull – he would certainly shake things up a bit as he grew in confidence and developed his own style. For now, though, he was not sure of his abilities. His self-doubt plagued him throughout his sermons and, along with the lack of an audience and growing criticism, he became convinced that he would be better off returning to teaching novitiates rather than preaching to the masses.

In 1485 things would change for him. He was ordered to go to San Gimignano, a neighbouring city in Tuscany, where he was to give the Lenten sermons. There he would learn the skills he would need to draw in an audience that would hang on his every word. Once those sermons were complete and he returned to Florence, nothing would ever be the same.

# Chapter 3

# The Hailstorm

Savonarola's sermons during his time in San Gimignano – with their portentous themes and ominous tones – were a prelude to the ones that he would later give in Florence. He told his congregations that the Church would be punished but would rise again. His time preaching in the Tuscan town changed the young preacher – he found his voice, and it was a voice that would shake Florence to its core. He must have been growing in confidence and his Lenten sermons must have been a success because he was invited back for the subsequent Lent.

In 1485, while in the walled town, he received a letter from his mother telling him that his father, Niccolò, had died. The news did not seem to affect Savonarola that much and in a reply to her, he stated that his father was Christ. But when, in October that year, he received news that his brother, Borso, had also died, he was somewhat affected by his mother's misery. His letter, written over several days, was much calmer though the words cannot have been much comfort to the grieving woman – he told her not to worry about his sisters and their poverty and to free herself from any such earthly concerns:

> I would wish you to be so much in love with Jesus that you care not for your children except in so far you are not able to do otherwise; I would wish your faith to be such that you could see them die and even martyred, like that saintly Jewish woman who saw her seven sons tortured and slain, without ever weeping; nay, rather did she comfort them to die.[1]

A year later, he was back in San Gimignano once again to preach the Lenten sermons. These included the first mention of his ideas of Church reform, and his words become more apocalyptic. For the first time, he also stated that he was not a prophet: 'We expect at any moment a scourge, or Antichrist, or war or plague or famine,' he said. 'If you ask me with Amos if I am a prophet I answer with him – I am not a prophet.'[2]

He gave eight reasons why this scourge would be coming to cleanse the Earth – the wickedness of men; the wicked shepherds given to the Church by God; because God sent his prophecy down to men (meaning Savonarola himself, which contradicted his earlier claims); because God had lost confidence in humanity; the decline of faith; the rotten core within the Church; the contempt of the saint and the growing lack of religious observances.

He continued to travel. In 1487 he made his way to Bologna where he taught at the university before returning to Ferrara the following year. Then he travelled to Brescia in Lombardy where he stayed for a number of years. He gave a sermon on St Andrew's Day in 1489 in which he used the Book of Revelations as his main theme. He spoke with a 'voice of thunder', telling the crowd of twenty-four elders of the apocalypse who sat around the throne of God, how he had received a vision of these celestial beings and how they told him Brescia would fall prey to a scourge, that blood would run through the streets and that children would be murdered in front of their parents' eyes.[3] The citizens of Brescia would come to remember these words when, in 1512, the town was invaded by the French Army who slaughtered the people and left them wading through blood in the streets. Some 6,000 infantry and 500 men at arms were led to the city by Gaston de Foix, and an assault was launched. The people desperately tried to defend their home – even women joined in the effort by flinging stones from walls onto the heads of their attackers.[4] But the defence was pointless. When a call for surrender was rejected, it left the city open to sacking.

Savonarola was back in Florence by 1490, at the behest of a man who would become the centerpiece of much of his ire – Lorenzo de' Medici. But it was a young man, Count Giovanni Pico della Mirandola, who convinced the ruler of Florence to bring Savonarola back. The young count was much admired by Lorenzo as well as by Savonarola himself. The two had first met during the friar's stay in Lombardy and Pico had been impressed with Savonarola's words[5] and the way he refused to hold back regarding the rampant corruption of the Church. It was the beginning of an unlikely friendship that would stay with both men until the end of their lives.

Nicknamed the 'Phoenix of Genius'[6], Giovanni Pico della Mirandola was born to Gianfrancesco Pico, Lord of Mirandola, and his wife Giulia. The family had close links to the Este family of Ferrara as well as the Sforza family of Milan – Pico came from a family of impeccable breeding. From an early age he was described as being particularly good-looking. His nephew, Giovanni Francesco Pico, describes him:

> He was of feature and shape feminine and beauteous, of stature goodly and high, of flesh tender and soft: his visage lovely and fair, his colour white intermingled with comely reds, his eyes grey and quick of look, his teeth white and even, his hair yellow and abundant.[7]

Mirandola, who was very fashionable but cared little about his unbrushed hair, was the opposite of Savonarola with his hard gaze, hooked nose and plain black Dominican robes. But like the friar, Pico was exceptionally intelligent and had learned Latin, Greek, Hebrew and Arabic at an early age. His interests were almost entirely philosophical, however, and he wished to understand from where the various religions that had brought Christianity into being had come. This mission would have him learning the ancient languages of Aramaic and Babylonian and he would end up being the only man in Europe able to understand them.[8] It is this exceptional understanding of religion and philosophy that ultimately drew Savonarola to the young count, despite their outward differences.

There was one particular event in Pico's life that certainly would have attracted the attention of the friar – just as it did Lorenzo de' Medici and myriad other individuals, not all of whom were as friendly. In 1486, he produced a huge text of 900 theological theses that covered a range of ideas, and said he would defend each and every single one in a philosophical debate in Rome with anyone who would question him.[9]

Mirandola aimed to spend a year in Rome expounding on his work and, according to just one of the many papal complaints made against him, he had posted copies of his tracts in public places in the city as well as having many more copies published in other parts of Europe. It was Mirandola's aim to gather as many experts for this debate as he could and so he sent copies of his work to all universities in Italy, and even offered to pay the travelling expenses for any expert to come to Rome.[10] He planned to host this great debate in front of Pope Innocent VIII. His Holiness was less than impressed. Innocent was the pope who, three years earlier, had endorsed the misogynistic ramblings of Kramer and Sprenger, two priests who wrote *Malleus Maleficarum* (the Hammer of the Witches) condemning women, in particular, to a grim and frightening fate at the hands of the Inquisition. It has been described as one of the most obscene books ever written. Innocent thought it was marvellous. Except the Pope took umbrage at Pico's work as many of the theses he proposed touched on astrology, attempted to reconcile Paganism with Christianity, and included points relating to the Kabbalah and the secrets of heavenly bodies. Seven of the theses were condemned by the Pope and, not wishing to irritate His Holiness, Pico quickly backed down. However, his *Apologia*, published in 1487, made things worse. In this work, he made clear his contempt of astrology, saying that the planets had absolutely no say in affecting the lives of people on Earth. Pope Innocent, a follower of astrology, condemned every point within it and threatened to excommunicate the young man unless he retracted everything that he had written.[11] Rather than once more bend to the Pope's will, Mirandola fled to France but was captured and held at Vincennes having been charged with heresy, only to be released in 1488 when Lorenzo de' Medici stepped in and convinced the Pope to drop the case against the young philosopher. Pico then decided to move to Florence, where he became part of Lorenzo's inner circle, and it was there that he once again came into contact with Girolamo Savonarola and persuaded the Medici patriarch to bring the friar, who had been preaching in Genoa following a tour of various Tuscan towns, back to the city.

Mirandola grew more pious over the years, disposed of much of his property and began to live less like the peacock he had been in his youth. Instead he devoted his time to study. A papal bull was even granted by Pope Alexander VI, forgiving Pico for his indiscretions against the previous pontiff.[12] Noticing that his dear friend had changed, Savonarola tried to have Pico join the Dominican Order. However, it was only when Mirandola lay on his deathbed that he agreed.

The friar was already making waves in the city, although it would be some time until he gained notoriety as a prophet. Upon his return to Florence, Savonarola began to lecture once more at San Marco. He taught logic to the novitiates but then, on a Sunday after Vespers, he would give talks in the cloisters, standing beneath a rose bush. His explanations of the scriptures were so popular among his brothers that he was asked to preach in the church attached to the convent – later moving into the gardens when the throng became bigger – and he soon proved he had found his voice. The once quiet young man, with his heavy Ferrarese accent, was now able to project to the back of the church – and when he preached, he did not hold back. There were no soft edges to the topics he chose to speak about and no leaning towards the increasingly popular Humanist teachings. Girolamo Savonarola preached as if he were the voice of God, and his bluntness started to win him favour amongst the citizens of Florence. He even described himself as 'the hailstorm that is going to smash the heads of those who do not take cover'.[13] A hailstorm he certainly was – his early sermons, just as the ones he gave on his visits to Ferrara and Brescia, concentrated on apocalyptic themes. They involved the need to reform the Church and punish it for its vices and corruption. It was his view that this corruption was a sword of Damocles hanging ominously above the heads of every Florentine citizen: 'Behold!' he said. 'The sword of the Lord will be over the Earth soon and swiftly.'[14]

He would return to the theme of vice again and again, particularly the vices of Florence and the selfishness of the ruling classes. And when he spoke of the ruling classes in Florence there could be no doubt who he was referring to – the 'prince' who was Lorenzo de' Medici. Initially, Lorenzo thought little of the attacks and found a lot to praise in the

Ferrarese friar's sermons, as the two men actually shared similar views in relation to the corrupt Church. However, they outraged those in the pro-Medicean circle, especially as the poor and dispossessed flocked to listen to him and applauded his onslaughts. To the hard-working poor and the peasants, this was a man who had come to their city and seen exactly what was wrong – and he was a man who would be able to fix it.

His popularity continued to grow, even with the ordinary citizens who, hypocritically, revelled in the vice-laden opportunities Florence had to offer: the city's gamblers, thieves, sodomites and bankers were his main targets. But Savonarola was walking on thin ice. Attacks on bankers displeased Lorenzo immensely and Pico della Mirandola warned him against speaking so harshly against de'Medici and his apparent corruption: 'You will come to no good end, jousting in this way,'[15] he said.

But the friar ignored his friend and continued to preach in an aggressive manner, and it was no secret against whom his ire was directed. As the argument between Savonarola and Lorenzo became more public, their behaviour in private was increasingly petty, such as when Savonarola made sure he was away from his cell in San Marco when Lorenzo visited the convent. Lorenzo tried to warn Savonarola to calm down, sending five of the city's most important men to talk with him during Easter of 1491, before he took to the pulpit in Florence's main cathedral. During this meeting, the friar turned to the men and, in an eerie prediction of their master's death, said, 'I'm here as a stranger and he's certainly the most important man in the city, yet I will remain and he will depart – I'm staying and he is going.'[16] He then sent the agents away.

In that Holy Week of 1491, as Savonarola stood before his congregation in his biggest venue yet, he launched a scathing attack on Lorenzo. He spoke of tyranny and denounced the bribery among members of the government. He likened the city to a modern-day Sodom and Gomorrah and called the Church the 'whore of Babylon'[17], returning repeatedly to the sin of sodomy. He warned that Florence would 'feel the edge of the sword' due to the heavy taxes that had been placed upon the poor while the nobility paid absolutely nothing. Savonarola's sermons attacked everything he saw as wrong with the city – and, although he never uttered his name, he put the responsibility of those wrongs down to the evils of Lorenzo de' Medici. To Savonarola, Lorenzo was nothing more than a dictator who was keeping the citizens of Florence from their rightful freedom. The man spent wantonly and, in his youth, had been well known for his indiscretions and his hedonism, and although he had mellowed as he had aged, that did not seem to matter to Savonarola. He preached to a full cathedral with a voice so powerful it could easily reach the back of the vast building. His confidence was growing and the sermons became far more daring in nature. This only made him more popular with the people and Girolamo Savonarola had the citizens of Florence in the palm of his hand.

Eventually, Lorenzo retaliated by asking Fra Mariano da Genazzano, a monk of the Augustinian order, to preach a counter sermon. It was a relatively tame move from Lorenzo, but it was cunning. In his younger days he probably would have tried something a little more ruthless but for now, this was the perfect way to bring Savonarola to heel. Instead of fighting fire with fire, he would fight friar with friar.

Fra Mariano was the polar opposite of Savonarola – whereas Savonarola's tone was brusque and apocalyptic, Mariano was calm and a man of the changing intellectual climate who had a love of classic poetry and pagan Classical learning. He was, at the time, the most celebrated preacher in Florence and almost everyone adored him. In fact, Lorenzo liked the Augustinian so much that he often invited him to stay at one of his country villas. It was during one of these visits that the poet Angelo Poliziano, a friend of both Lorenzo and Pico della Mirandola, wrote of him:

I have met Fra Mariano repeatedly at the villa and entered into confidential talks with him. I never knew a man at once more attractive and more cautious. He neither repels by immoderate severity nor deceives and leads astray by exaggerated indulgence.[18]

He spoke with such grace and composure it impressed many in Florence, including a number of monks from San Marco. One of them, Domenico

Benivieni, contacted Savonarola and said: 'Father there is no denying that your doctrine is true, useful and necessary, but your way of delivering it lacks grace, especially when it is so frequently compared to that of Fra Mariano.'[19]

Mariano's sermon was to take place in the Church of Santo Spirito, attached to the Monastery of San Gallo on Ascension Day in 1491. This meant there would be enough distance between Savonarola's Lenten sermon so it would not simply look like a personal attack on the Dominican. Unfortunately for Mariano, it turned into just that and ended up harming both him and his reputation.

The opinion that Mariano was a good man and an even better preacher was shared by many. Yet this counterattack on Savonarola would result in his losing his foothold. He simply could not hide his jealousy and animosity towards his rival. As he spoke, rather than maintaining his usual calm demeanour, he lost his temper and unleashed a scorching personal attack on Savonarola, accusing him of being a false prophet. If the sermon was meant to turn people away from the Dominican, it did not work. Instead, the congregation was so shocked by Mariano's performance that they became curious about the friar who had inspired such rage in the usually calm preacher, and went to his sermons to see what all the fuss was about.

By this point, the health of the great Lorenzo de' Medici was failing and it soon became clear to him, and his family, that Florence's leader was dying. His son Giovanni, who had been accepted into the College of Cardinals, stopped off to see his father before he left for Rome. He was presented with a letter warning him to be careful as the world he was about to enter was 'a sink of all iniquities'.[20] The letter contained instructions for Giovanni to live a pious life, but also a warning – Lorenzo knew of the corruption that existed within the walls of the Vatican and wanted his son to be prepared.

Lorenzo went to his villa at Careggi in March 1492 and strange omens occurred soon after. Just two weeks after his arrival, news reached him that the city's famous lions had mauled each other to death. Shortly after that, a huge storm hit Florence and lightning struck one of the lanterns that adorned the dome of the cathedral dislodging one of the marble balls. Lorenzo asked which side of the cathedral the ball had fallen on and when he was advised that it was the north-western side, he announced sombrely: 'Ah well, I shall die; it fell on the side nearest my house.'[21]

Death was indeed coming for the patriarch of the Medici family. But as he lay dying, surrounded by family, he made the shocking decision to summon Girolamo Savonarola to his bedside.

The men had a long meeting, just the two of them, and it is unclear exactly what was said. Many legends persist around the conversation. One, written by a supporter of Savonarola, states that the friar demanded certain conditions of the dying man before he would even think about giving absolution; firstly that Lorenzo must have faith in the Lord God, to which the dying man said he did; secondly that he must make restitution for everything that had unjustly been taken by his family, to which Lorenzo agreed.[22] But when the third was given, that Lorenzo restore Florence to liberty, de' Medici fell silent and refused to answer. Poliziano mentions this in his own writings and says that as Savonarola was leaving, Lorenzo begged the friar to give him absolution, which was gladly given. Some versions state that the dying man was not given absolution at all. What we do know is that Lorenzo found great comfort in Savonarola's visit. He died just a few days later on 8 April 1492. Poliziano gives an account of Lorenzo's final moments, including how he managed to joke about his own death:

> When given something to eat and asked how he liked it he replied, 'As well as a dying man can like anything.' He embraced us all tenderly and humbly asked pardon if during his illness he had caused annoyance to anyone. Then disposing himself to receive extreme unction he commended his soul to God.[23]

Lorenzo de' Medici, prince in all but name, was buried in the Church of San Lorenzo in the family chapel next to the tomb of his murdered brother, Giuliano. His death left Florence in the hands of his son, Piero. The people were understandably worried for their future as Piero had little talent for politics. Change was coming and it would be headed by the black-robed figure of Girolamo Savonarola.

# Chapter 4

# Lorenzo de' Medici

Lorenzo de' Medici was born on 1 January 1449, at least according to the modern calendar. The Florentine calendar has Lorenzo born in 1448, as its new year began on 5 March, the Feast of the Annunciation. Five days later he was baptised publicly at the baptistery of San Giovanni in Florence. The ceremony was attended by some of the most important men in the city, with the Archbishop of Florence even standing as godfather to the young Medici heir.

The child grew up in the magnificent Palazzo Medici which at the time was still being built. The palazzo, just a stone's throw from the Cathedral of Santa Maria del Fiore, was an utterly magnificent building which exuded power and driving ambition. The palace would remain Lorenzo's home until his death, but the Medici family did not always stay within the hustle and bustle of the city. Cosimo de' Medici, Lorenzo's grandfather, owned a number of properties in the Tuscan countryside, including a villa at nearby Careggi. This villa would become one of Lorenzo's favourite getaways. Cosimo could often be found working in the gardens there – a serene environment that was different from the fast-paced political hubbub of the city. Other countryside retreats included the villas of Cafaggiolo and Trebbio, both of which lay within the Medici ancestral homeland of the Mugello.

The palazzo on the corner of Via Larga was much smaller in Lorenzo's day than the building which attracts tourists today. It was expanded in the seventeenth century by the Riccardi family, which is why today it is known as Palazzo Medici-Riccardi. The rooms would have been full of opulent decorations and furniture. The collection of art and beautiful objects which had been started by Cosimo de' Medici and carried on by his grandson would become world famous. Visiting the Medici palazzo,

Galeazzo Maria Sforza was astounded by the extensive collection and one of his staff members recounted his master's awe:

> [We] went on a tour of this palace, and especially of its noblest parts, such as some studies, little chapels, living rooms, bedchambers and gardens, all of which are constructed with admirable skill, embellished on every side with gold and fine marbles, with carvings and sculptures in relief, with pictures and inlays done in perspective by the most accomplished and perfect of masters.[1]

The young Lorenzo would have watched in wonder as the palazzo took shape, in particular, the beautiful family chapel. It was painted with frescoes by Benozzo Gozzoli depicting the Adoration of the Magi, a subject that was very close to the entire Medici family. Visitors to the chapel today are overwhelmed by the beauty of these frescoes as the story unfolds in a complete 360 degrees. And painted within the frescoes are members of the Medici family – Cosimo is sitting on a donkey, while Lorenzo is seen within the crowds following the young magus, Caspar. The journey twists its way through the Tuscan countryside with numerous painted castles based closely on Medici properties. Other allies of the family are also portrayed, including the very important Duke of Milan, Galeazzo Maria Sforza. The frescoes span the entirety of the chapel and represent the journey of the Magi towards the birthplace of Christ and onwards to a heavenly goal. But they also represent just how close the Medici believed themselves to be to the Magi. The beginning of the journey, for instance, shows fortifications similar to those of Cafaggiolo and Trebbio, while mixing in imagery of Jerusalem and the Holy Land. This represents where the Magi were summoned to see King Herod before they began their journey to find the Christ child.

The landscape is dotted with throwbacks to places that the Medici had visited, or simply travelled past, on their journeys around the Tuscan countryside. The western wall seems to represent the Mugello. This wilderness is where the Medici originated from, and the area continued to be an important power base for the family.[2]

Lorenzo was raised to be a ruler and it was something the people swiftly backed. As a member of the Medici family, and more importantly an heir of 'Piero the Gouty', the boy found himself being inundated with requests for patronage. As someone of status, from the ruling family, it was believed that Lorenzo could open doors for people. He took to this job with gusto, delivering results and putting in a good word with his father where he could. In fact he did so well that his father often used him for important business trips, knowing that his son could charm those he came into contact with. One such example was in 1463, when Lorenzo was sent to Pistoia. He certainly made a good impression, but it also became clear even this early on that Lorenzo de' Medici liked to have fun, with a love of art, festivities, fine dining and beautiful women. As he rose in prominence and gained more political power, he became more visible publicly, while his father remained more often than not in his sickbed (he suffered terribly from gout). But unlike the rest of his family, who were graced with good looks, Lorenzo wasn't exactly the most handsome of men.

Portraits of Lorenzo, even those painted posthumously, show a man with a flattened nose, which apparently had no sense of smell, a heavy jaw that jutted forward when he spoke and irregularly shaped eyebrows.[3] Yet despite his less than stellar looks, Lorenzo de' Medici still attracted the ladies. When he spoke his face became animated and his dark eyes were full of insight and shone with utter joy. He was also athletic – he played a form of football with twenty-seven players on each side, and enjoyed hunting, hawking and jousting – and the opposite sex could not get enough of him. He was educated, loved books (his book collection along with his array of antique sculptures was the envy of Italy), sang – despite his nasal voice – and had a preference for sexual innuendo, bawdy stories and practical jokes. Mixed in with this fun-loving side, he was kind and compassionate with a deep-seated love of animals. Who could possibly dislike such a man?

Lorenzo certainly did not let his growing political work get in the way of his social life. During a period of unrest with the Party on the Hill in 1467 – when the leading members were exiled following a period of violence with their enemies, the Party of the Plains in 1465/66 – those who had been banished wanted their revenge. They began to plan a war, which involved the use of mercenaries and bandits in order to kidnap or murder the Medici heir. However, at the same time, Lorenzo had, coincidentally, decided to take himself off to the spa at Bagno a Morba. This trip served two purposes – firstly to have fun, and secondly because, like his father, he suffered with gout. The waters of the spa were thought to help alleviate the excruciating pains it caused, and trips there were commonplace. As he was out of town when the bandits were heading his way, this sojourn might also have saved his life.

Lorenzo spent much of his spare time outside the city in the family villas of Careggi and Fiesole with his circle of friends discussing poetry, art and philosophy. He was particularly learned in Humanism and enjoyed spending time with those who could understand the Bible and discuss Aristotle, along with other Classical philosophy. It was during these stays at the family villas that Lorenzo began to write his own poetry, having been heavily influenced by the work of diplomat and poet Luigi Pulci. They became good friends and Pulci would spend a lot of time with him and, later, his family. He was known in particular for his work *Morgante*, a poem that told the romantic tale of Orlando and Renaud de Montauban in a burlesque fashion. It was full of humour and strange adventures, such as when one character is killed by a crab bite and another literally dies laughing. This style of writing influenced Lorenzo in his own verses.

But the fun could not last forever as adult life was about to take over. As Piero's health grew worse, it became increasingly important that Lorenzo should get married. Normally the families of high-born men and women looked within Florence for their children's prospective spouses, but Lorenzo's parents were about to go completely against the norm. Lorenzo's mother, Lucrezia Tornabuoni, began searching in Rome for the woman who would marry her son. She settled on the Orsini family, who were exceptionally powerful in Rome, with members on the highest rungs of the Church ladder. Marrying into the Orsinis would enable the Medici to extend their political reach, even if it did put the noses of Florentine nobles out of joint. The young woman chosen was Clarice Orsini, and in 1467 Lucrezia travelled to Rome to get a good look at her. She reported:

> She is fairly tall and fair skinned. She is gentle in manner without the sophistication of a Florentine but she should be easy to train ... . Her face is on the round side, but pleasant enough ... . I could not judge her breasts, for the Romans keep theirs well covered, but they appeared to be well formed.[4]

It sounds as though Lucrezia was shopping at a cattle market, which is not far from the truth. The bride had to be perfect. Not only did she have to bring a powerful alliance and a good dowry – and be good-looking – she had to be able to continue the Medici line. A further meeting between Lucrezia and Clarice showed the Medici matriarch that her prospective daughter-in-law was rather shy. Not that it mattered to Lucrezia. But Lorenzo showed little interest in the woman who would become his wife, preferring to spend his time with his amours. Nevertheless, he agreed. He knew a wife's only real use to him would be to provide children and he could seek emotional and sexual fulfilment, and perhaps love, elsewhere.

Some of the highest-ranking Florentine families were seriously offended by the fact the Medici heir was marrying a girl from outside the city. To help smooth things over, a huge tournament was organised, which involved jousting, an activity Lorenzo enjoyed, despite not being particularly skilled in its execution. It was to be a magnificent affair costing a large amount of money. The competitors were made up of some of the most eligible, and reckless, young Florentine men who paraded themselves in the Piazza Santa Croce on the day of the tournament, 7 February 1469, dressed to the nines in ostentatious armour for themselves, and their horses. The queen of the tournament was Lucrezia Donati, who was said to be one of the most beautiful women in the city, and who was also Lorenzo's mistress. Of course Lorenzo, who was the most magnificently dressed of all the competitors, won the day by default rather than any skill, although even he graciously admitted that.

Four months after the tournament, Clarice Orsini arrived in Florence for her wedding. Celebrations began in earnest – five massive banquets were thrown in the Palazzo Medici and presents were showered on the young couple. For three days the palazzo was full of friends and family as they celebrated the nuptials. But despite the families' joy at the union, it soon became clear that Lorenzo and Clarice were not the best match. Lorenzo spent most of his time pining over his mistress, Lucrezia Donati, while Clarice earned a reputation for being haughty and rude. As an outsider in Florence, she spent her time looking down on everyone disapprovingly, as if from the top of a pedestal of Roman nobility. Nevertheless, there must have been some sexual attraction between the two as they would go on to have ten children, and they did seem to have mutual affection for one another.

On 2 December 1469, Piero died at the villa of Careggi. Power passed to Lorenzo, who at barely 20 years of age, was reluctant to take on such a heavy burden. Lorenzo records in his diaries that two days after his father's death, a delegation of men, headed by his uncle Tommaso Soderini, was received at the Palazzo Medici in order to formally place control of the city in Lorenzo's hands. After the meeting he wrote:

> The second day after my father's death, although I, Lorenzo, was very young, being only twenty years of age, the principal men of the city and of the State came to us ... to encourage me to take charge of the city and of the state, as my grandfather and father had done. This I did, though on account of my youth and the great responsibility and perils arising therefrom, with great reluctance, solely for the safety of our friends and of our possessions.[5]

It did not take long for Lorenzo to become embroiled in bitter events that would test the young man's leadership skills, such as when he had to step in and calm issues between Naples and Milan, the latter of which was Florence's closest ally. In late December 1469, ambassadors from both cities were called to Florence to resolve their differences, but the meeting ended with insults being thrown. The relationship between the city states soon got worse and in March 1470, Galeazzo Maria Sforza of Milan responded to rumours of Ferrante of Naples being in secret talks with Venice by withdrawing his ambassadors. In April, the Neapolitans did exactly the same thing. This left Florence with a sour taste in its mouth and Lorenzo slap bang in the middle of a government split between supporting Naples and Milan.

He found himself leaning heavily on his uncle, Tommaso Soderini which, with the benefit of hindsight, was very naïve. Soderini had quickly become one of Lorenzo's most trusted advisors and many believed that, at this early stage, he was the true power behind Lorenzo's throne. He was a highly respected man but he was also feared and hated. It was said that he sauntered about Florence with 'honey in his mouth and a knife on his belt'.[6] He certainly did not use his position to help his nephew; rather he used the collapse of the alliance with Naples and Milan to gain more influence over Lorenzo and tried desperately to have his nephew support the Neapolitan cause. Lorenzo, however, was not willing to give up his closest ally, although he had to be careful with Naples in order to bring them back on side.

Soderini's influence was such that he was managing to edge Lorenzo and the Signoria (the governing authority) ever closer to Naples. He got hold of a number of letters from the Neapolitan envoy, Otto Niccolini, hinting that they would be leaving Florence in the lurch for Venice. He called a *practica*, or meeting of the government, to discuss important issues, which was organised so secretly that the Milanese officials had no idea it was even happening until it was over. Even Lorenzo was left behind and almost missed the meeting, only finding out about it after it had begun. Lorenzo later admitted to Sforza that by the time he arrived, the *practica* was already completed and there was nothing he could do to fix it. It was a wake-up call for the young leader of Florence, and he decided to use his political wiles and play for time. When Ferrante of Naples demanded that Lorenzo openly declare for the southern state, Lorenzo dithered and caused no end of delays, eventually managing to convince the Signoria that they should not accept any deal from Naples until it had been agreed with the Duke of Milan.

Despite this being a victory for Lorenzo, Soderini still had a few tricks up his sleeve. The atmosphere in Florence was tense and so another *practica* was called for 27 June. This time, however, Lorenzo was to prove he was much more astute, and that he had learned a difficult lesson following the last meeting the previous month. He ensured that this *practica* was dominated by men loyal to him, and they succeeded in shouting down their rivals who were headed by Soderini. Those unsure of who to side with were swiftly convinced to join Lorenzo and so overwhelming was the support for him that Soderini and his cronies agreed not to finalise a separate treaty with Naples. To make matters worse – and much better for Lorenzo – Venice rejected Ferrante's request for an alliance. Then, on 12 July, Lorenzo reported that Naples had agreed to re-join the alliance between Florence and Milan, and it was followed by the Duke and Duchess of Milan visiting the city in 1471.

Now it was time for him to really take control of the city. In the past, the government of Florence had been an entity that could easily overthrow the Medici, as had been proven in 1466 when Piero de' Medici had almost been toppled. It was time to rework the Council of One Hundred, an important governmental body, created in 1458, which had much of the power and was full of some of the most ambitious men in the city. These men were as likely to side against the Medici as support them. Not only that, but a select group of the council, the Accoppiatori, had control over the electoral process. So if they did not want a group of Lorenzo's supporters in power, they could put a stop to it quickly. Thus Lorenzo used his political and persuasive power (mainly bribery) to reform the council and Accoppiatori. The reform was pushed through quickly and it was agreed that the Accoppiatori would be selected annually by those who were leaving the current government. This was a clever move by Lorenzo and his supporters – the Signoria was a system of government that excluded the majority of citizens from serving, so bringing in this new set up meant it would be a closed loop and would always be full of men whom Lorenzo trusted. Even better for the head of the Medici family, a new council was created – the Council of Forty was a permanent group within the Council of One Hundred made up almost entirely of

Lorenzo's friends. By bringing in these reforms, Lorenzo de' Medici did what his grandfather and father could not – he turned the government of Florence into a well-oiled machine that worked alongside the republican system. More importantly, it meant that nothing could be passed in government without his approval.

Rebellion was still rife, particularly in the early days when Lorenzo was trying to prove himself worthy of ruling. Just four months after coming to power, he faced a challenge in the town of Prato. Following a previous rebellion, Lorenzo's father had banished Bernardo Nardi, who had marched a small army into Prato before going straight for Florence and attempting a coup. This was dealt with easily by the town's mayor, Cesare Petrucci, who rounded up Nardi and his co-conspirators and had them summarily executed. Of course, Petrucci would be well-rewarded for his role in extinguishing the rebellion before the militia of Florence could even arrive to help.

However, not every fight would be so easy for Lorenzo. A storm was brewing between the Medici and the papacy. The Medici family had long been a banking family and had once been one of the largest banks in Europe, with branches stretching from Italy to France and even to England. But by the time Lorenzo took power, the bank was failing. His father had little interest in banking, preferring to spend his time collecting art and jewels and running the city. Still, the family bank had, for a long time, been in control of the papal finances and Lorenzo intended to carry on that tradition. After Pope Paul II died on 26 July 1471, Cardinal Francesco della Rovere was elected Pope Sixtus IV. Unlike popes before and after him, Sixtus had achieved the position through sheer hard work and many were hopeful that he would not be quite so corrupt and could put in place some actual reforms. Just after the Pope's election, Lorenzo was asked to visit Rome with a number of other delegates in order to congratulate him. Once there, Sixtus greeted him warmly and agreed to keep the papal bank accounts in Medici control. But the good feelings were not to last.

When Sixtus selected a bride for his nephew, Girolamo Riario, he decided that he wanted a wedding gift for the couple and approached the Medici bank for a loan to buy the town of Imola. Lorenzo was not keen, as he had been eyeing the little town for himself, and so refused the request. Rather than just simply finding another wedding gift for his nephew, Sixtus went to the Medici's banking rivals, the Pazzi. It is easy to imagine how pleased they would have been to grant the request, ecstatic to have trumped the Medici in this way. Still smarting from the refusal of the loan, Sixtus also snubbed Lorenzo's brother for a cardinal's hat despite promising him the post, thus ending their relationship for good. This would lead to one of the greatest crises of Lorenzo's political career as well as deep personal tragedy.

A conspiracy was forming at the hands of the Pazzi, who believed the Medici family had achieved too much power and that Lorenzo was too tyrannical in his rule. They wanted the Medici ousted so that they could take their place, so they hatched the plot to have Lorenzo and his brother Giuliano killed. As we have noted, the deed took place during Mass on 26 April 1478. Lorenzo survived but Giuliano was stabbed several times and left to die on the floor of the cathedral. The reprisals were tough – Lorenzo hunted down those who murdered his brother, executing them without a second thought. The Pazzi family were in disgrace thanks to their role in the conspiracy – not only were Jacopo and Francesco de' Pazzi executed, but members of the family left behind were forced into exile. Their coat of arms were destroyed and their property confiscated.

Lorenzo and the Signoria took a hard line with those who conspired to overthrow the Medici and while this was seen as tyrannical by some, Lorenzo had now cemented himself as the actual ruler of Florence, and his position was undisputed. He would go on to prove himself time and time again, while many citizens grumbled that they wanted the republic back as it had been before the Medici had taken over.

It would fall to the unassuming Dominican friar who set foot in the city in 1481 to help remove the Medici from power, and return the city to its republican past.

# Chapter 5

# Divisions

Florence was no stranger to division. It had already seen how one man and one political regime could divide the citizens in such a way that chaos could sometimes ensue. It was no different with Girolamo Savonarola. His puritanical beliefs meant that the city should be free of vice and corruption and its people should lead simple lives, following God's word with no gambling, no prostitution, no ostentation – the opposite of fun-loving Lorenzo's. There were two main factions that supported Savonarola – the Frateschi and the Piagnoni. The Frateschi ('the friar's men') were made up of the monks of San Marco as well as Savonarola's intellectual friends, such as Pico della Mirandola and Giovanni Nesi, a Humanist who served as gonfalonier twice during his life, and who wrote a number of works praising the friar. His best-known work reflecting his Savonarolan views was *Oraculum de novo Saeculo* written in 1497. It announced the advent of a new kingdom, a new Jerusalem, in Florence, as had been prophesied by Savonarola. Nesi heralded this as a return to a golden age and praised Savonarola. He wrote of the coming of a 'Socrates from Ferrara'[1] – an obvious reference to the humble friar. He went on to say that this Socrates will, 'Brighten the earth … open to all the font of truth … all, finally, will follow [him].'[2]

The oraculum was well received by Savonarolan supporters and they compared Nesi favourably with other authors who had written in Savonarola's defence. At the same time, and as was expected, many anti-Savonarolans spoke out against Nesi, fearing his work was evidence that he had lost his way, and they tried to call him back onto what they believed was the right path. One such detractor, Giovanni Caroli, was a member of Savonarola's own Dominican Order and was based at Santa Maria Novella, a short walk from San Marco. He wrote to Nesi and told him that he had gone too far in praising the prior of San Marco and that he preached against Florentine morals. His anger was evident:

> Harshest castigator of the vices, gravest praiser of the virtues: What a bombastic name! What a presumptuous sentiment! What vain praise and most prideful pride! So, Florence has come to such a point of poverty that it is necessary to accept in turn this new 'Socrates' from the swamps of Ferrara![3]

Caroli was obviously afraid of Savonarola; aware that his power could be dangerous, and his attack on Nesi compounded the fact that he thought excessive praise could also be dangerous. Still, Caroli's words fell on deaf ears and Nesi continued to support the prior of San Marco. Undeterred, he published a number of leaflets that showed Savonarola as a false prophet who was destroying the Church and failing in his duty as a holy man.

The Piagnoni, meaning 'the grumblers', were made up of more simple folk – the poorer citizens who still held a deep-seated hatred of the Medici family. There were also opposition parties that were created out of dislike – often hatred – of what Savonarola was doing, and his censorious attitude. The largest of these were the Bigi, who plotted for the return of the Medici, and another was the Arrabbiati, meaning 'the enraged ones', who also wished to see the return of the family. As did the Compagnacci, or 'the rowdy ones'. There were also smaller groups – the Bianchi ('the whites') were made up of individuals who, although pleased to see the end of Medicean rule, rather missed the freedom that they had under Lorenzo the Magnificent; a freedom they certainly would not get from Savonarola. Another of the smaller factions were the Tiepidi – meaning 'the tepid ones', moderate in their political views. This group was popular among the wealthy families and members of the clergy who believed that they should not have to live in poverty, as the godly Savonarola insisted. This group also had close links with Rome and Alexander VI, who would become one of Savonarola's greatest enemies.[4] This multitude of groups caused great divisions in Florence, as the historian Francesco Guicciardini noted: 'In the public councils one faction fought against the other, and as happens in divided cities, no man thought of the common good, so intent was he upon smashing his adversary's reputation.'[5]

However, followers of the prior of San Marco outnumbered his dissenters and Savonarola did not just have these groups on his side offering support from a distance, he also had a secret weapon known as the Fanciulli – a group of boys known for their unruliness. The friar employed them to shout insults at gamblers or overdressed women, and go into the taverns to reprimand drunkards. These rowdy young men had once been involved in the famous carnival fights on the city streets in which rocks were thrown, but now they collected alms and patrolled the streets singing hymns, insulting gamblers and drinkers and bringing the citizens into God's embrace. This youthful army was chosen by Savonarola at an impressionable age so that he could expose them to his religious ideals before they reached the age of reason and, in many cases, before they had reached puberty. Could this be because he believed they were more pure? Indeed, Fra Domenico later commented that the leaders of this army of boys were chosen 'not so much for their age as purity of life and natural judgment'.[6] Despite the fact that they had once been unruly little vagabonds, being chosen by Savonarola cast them in a new light and many saw them as 'an uncorrupted and incorruptible youth brigade'.[7]

Savonarola argued that he was saving these young men from the sin of prostitution and sodomy. After all, it was well known just how popular young boys were in the Florentine prostitution market. Sodomy was a particular sin that Savonarola could not tolerate – not only did he preach against it from the pulpit, but he urged the government to pass a law making it punishable by death. The vote was passed in a landslide in December 1494, and those accused and found guilty were executed in the most horrendous of ways – they would hang first and then be burned.[8] It is ironic that the man who brought this vicious punishment into the statutes would later face it himself.

Savonarola inspired feelings of hatred amongst those who stood against him and there were many attempts to discredit him throughout his time in Florence. For example, in 1495 Gonfalonier Filippo Corbizzi invited Savonarola to the Palazzo della Signoria for a debate, but when he arrived, he found himself surrounded by many of his enemies including two of his most outspoken critics – Fra Tommaso da Rieti and Fra Domenico da Ponzo. Domenico had, at one point, sung Savonarola's praises and insisted that his prophecies would come true. But then he had changed his mind and had started denouncing Savonarola as a fraud. In the palazzo, and surrounded by his enemies, Savonarola was asked to explain why he had dared to interfere in matters of state. After all, it was not his place to do so. His prophecies were also called into question. He refused to answer, saying that his prophecies would be justified to the masses once they came true, and that he would answer their questions at some point in the future. And in true Savonarola style, he answered his critics from the pulpit.

He told the Florentines that they deserved their newfound freedom from tyranny and the Medici. His promise that he would do anything to make sure they kept that freedom was well received and boosted his popularity. It must be said that despite his hardline beliefs, he did a lot of good for Florence. While some of his rules may seem harsh from a modern standpoint, he made sure that the city was kept as free from crime as possible by imposing the harshest of sentences. He also had a hand in the total reform of the Florentine government – he was hugely in favour of the new Grand Council, a group of men who had taken over from the Medici rule.

In the imposing fortress of the Palazzo della Signoria is a large chamber known as the Salone dei Cinquecento or Hall of the Five Hundred. This space, fifty-four metres long, twenty-three metres wide and eighteen metres high, was commissioned by Savonarola in 1494, and the work was completed by Simone del Pollaiuolo and Francesco Domenico. But the opulent hall that we see today was not how it was originally. When it was built, the room was very basic and devoid of any sort of decoration, reflecting Savonarola's views on ostentation. Eventually, however, the hall was decorated at the behest of Piero Soderini, who was given the title of gonfalonier for life in 1502, and Soderini commissioned Michelangelo and Leonardo da Vinci to work on two huge murals. Da Vinci worked on a piece based on the Battle of Anghiari, while Michelangelo's painting depicted the Battle of Cascina. Both battles were very important to

Florence's history as they demonstrated the city's might and valour. The Battle of Anghiari took place on 29 June 1440 and was fought between Milan and Florence – it was a victory for the Florentines and meant that they had full control over central Italy. Yet the battle is famous for one thing in particular – despite lasting all day and being fought between thousands of men, legend has it that only one man was killed after he fell off his horse. The Battle of Cascina took place on 28 July 1364 and was one of many contests between Pisa and Florence in the fight for Pisan freedom. It was a huge victory for Florence and the Pisan Army suffered a large number of losses, both in deaths and in prisoners being taken. Alas, neither was ever produced. Da Vinci's mural was the only one that was started and it soon became clear that it was a disaster. Da Vinci was known for trying out new techniques and this one was no different; he tried to apply oil paints to a thick undercoat, which made the paint drip. Despite his best efforts, the painting could not be saved. Michelangelo only ever completed the initial cartoons for his murals, but these were destroyed by one of his rivals in a fit of jealousy.

It was only under the return of the Medici that the room became decorated with the beautiful paintings seen today, paintings completed by the Renaissance master and author of *Lives of the Artists*, Giorgio Vasari.

In a way this chamber can be compared with modern parliaments – perhaps a Renaissance version of the House of Commons – and there are many who have argued that Savonarolan Florence was the birthplace of the modern political party. However, historian and author Lauro Martines argues that we must be careful with this viewpoint – after all, the Republic of Florence did not deal in democracy in the same way we do today. Despite not being ruled over by one man, the Grand Council was still split into factions and immersed in hierarchy. Family groups and petty arguments, something that had been prominent in previous governments, still held sway.[9] Paul Strathern also notes, interestingly, that family ties and loyalty were more important in the new government than anything else, just as they always had been. Additionally, if anyone were to speak out against any government policy then they would be arrested, placed in prison or exiled.[10] Despite this, in the eyes of Savonarola as well as many of the citizens, this was still better than the corrupt and tyrannical rule of the Medici.

For now, Florence was putty in his hands. Savonarola made sure that the citizens who crowded outside the cathedral during his sermons knew that they had helped Florence take the place of Rome as the most holy Christian city. His aim was to reform the Catholic Church and to do that he would start with Florence; he would turn it into a city where everyone lived according to God's word. And to many, the friar's word was absolute law. While the city was still divided, the large number of followers were not violent towards the pro-Medicean sympathisers that still lived in Florence. Instead, they worked towards making sure that Medicean policies were got rid of completely – for instance, the calling of *parlamenti* (the calling of citizens allowed to 'vote' via the ringing of the *vacca*) was completely scrapped. Why? Because they argued the government was in the hands of the people, so there was no need for one. After all, those who had called *parlamenti* in the past had been the nobility. Such a thing was not needed any more. And, for now, these types of changes were popular enough – Guicciardini stated in his *History of Italy* that he approved of the alterations, especially as Savonarola had managed to convince the republic to act on his suggestions without any violence whatsoever. Guicciardini added, however:

> Since such matters could not have been deliberated without the consent of many who were very suspect in memory of things past, it was decided that for the present, the Grand Council be set up as the foundation of their new won freedom, postponing to remedy what was lacking for a better occasion when those who at present were not capable of knowing, by reason and judgement, what was good for the public welfare, would by experience come to know it.[11]

Guicciardini, a man who lived through Savonarolan rule in Florence, had the foresight to know that while he and many others agreed with the changes in government, bringing in such democracy could end up bringing about the return of the Medici amidst violence and bloodshed.

The historian was perhaps beginning to think that everything within Florence was too good to be true.

In all the changes on the Florentine political stage, Savonarola managed to convince himself that Charles VIII of France, who invaded Italy in 1494, would be a new Cyrus who would turn Florence into a new Jerusalem. He had wished to cleanse Rome of Rodrigo Borgia, Alexander VI, and believed wholeheartedly that when Charles VIII left Florence and marched to the Eternal City that he would depose him. Disappointment came, however, when Charles left Rome without incident. But Savonarola had not given up hope, even going so far as to write letters to the French king in which he claimed, unequivocally, to be a prophet. He told the king proudly that Florence had taken the place of Rome as God's Holy City where her people lived without the vice and corruption that littered the streets of Rome. But Charles never once bothered to answer his letters. The friar was met with stony silence. Not that it seemed to matter to Savonarola – he had more important things to do, such as making sure *his* city became the perfect Godly city, free from the tyrants who had been so recently ejected. The Signoria agreed with him and, in October 1496, Donatello's sculpture of *Judith and Holofernes*, in which she cuts off his head, was moved from the Medici Palace gardens into the Palazzo della Signoria. It was placed there as an example of tyrannicide, which the city did not wish to see within its walls again.

There can be no doubt that Savonarola approved of the political changes that were happening within Florence. After all, he had been one of the main catalysts for removing the Medici from power. With the Grand Council now in place, it was time for the government to look at and reform other policies. One of the first to come into question was that of the 'twenty electors', a group of men who had been elected to control what happened within Florence in one of the final *parlamenti* in 1494. Their powers included being able to elect the Signoria, which paved the way for resentment. After all, if these men had the power to elect, who was to say they would not block their enemies from gaining one of the coveted places? Not only that, but the twenty came from the higher echelons of

Florentine society, a tier which many now believed should not be there at all. So the twenty had to go. By 7 June 1495, every member had resigned.[12]

Another policy that gained the ire of Savonarola and his supporters was that of the 'six beans'. The six beans was the Signoria's way of condemning a citizen to death, exile or some other such punishment, or letting the accused person go. Within this voting system, the black beans stood for a yes vote and the white for no – and the vote could only pass with a two-thirds majority. Except, as the Signoria did not comprise a court of law and held only six men, they basically wielded unchecked power. In exceptional circumstances the voting was scrapped and the Signoria acted in the same way an emperor would. This harked back to Roman law and had not been challenged until Savonarola took it upon himself to question it. In essence, they had absolute power over a person's fate in certain situations, which Savonarola believed was not right as Florence was now a city in which all citizens should be equal. Left to their own devices, the Signoria and their six beans could well be a dictatorship. Savonarola proposed that a new law be established, in which the condemned citizen could go above the Signoria and appeal to the Grand Council. This was, of course, resented by Savonarola's political opponents, but the law granting right of appeal was passed by the Grand Council, thus depriving the Signoria of their unchecked power.[13] It was a huge victory for Savonarola.

Despite his successes, this opposition was dangerous, especially from those who had links to the Church that he had spoken against so brazenly. Getting on the wrong side of the Pope was a bad idea. Alexander VI had already tried to summon Savonarola to Rome to explain himself, but Savonarola had refused the invitation over and over again. He came up with myriad excuses, even citing a violent attack on his person as a reason why he could not go. He argued that going outside without a bodyguard could very well end in disaster. This belief was one of the few he shared with Lorenzo de' Medici, who took an armed guard everywhere with him following the Pazzi conspiracy. Savonarola's refusal to listen to the pope would ultimately prove to be his undoing – Alexander VI was a ruthless man who would not put up with any form of dissent against his rule or his papacy.

Even though danger surrounded him, Savonarola was at the height of his power. He held sway over the people of Florence spiritually and politically. The Florentine government, the Grand Council, went to him for practically everything. At this stage in his life, he could do no wrong – the citizens loved him, and they listened to him. They were pulled in like fish on a hook, attracted by his exceptional oratory and the way he twisted philosophy and religion together to convince the people that he was a prophet, sent to turn Florence into a new Jerusalem. Savonarola was an intelligent man who had studied the works of Humanist scholars and ancient philosophers, working them into his sermons. Through these speeches, he made it clear that he believed the human race knew the world through the evidence of their own senses – a Humanist ideal first put forward by Aristotle and St Thomas Aquinas.[14] His rhetoric continued to win him far more supporters than opponents and Savonarola was, to all intents and purposes, the head of the city of Florence. It was a dangerous place to be, as previous leaders had seen. But for now, Girolamo Savonarola was quite happy where he was and believed that he could do absolutely anything.

# Chapter 6

# The Expulsion of the Medici

Piero de' Medici was the first living son born to Lorenzo and Clarice on 15 February 1472. Previous sons had died – twins born in 1471 only lived long enough to be baptised – so Piero was the heir, the one who would take over from his father and eventually run Florence. He was joined by a number of other siblings – his elder sister Lucrezia was born in 1470 and another sister, Maddalena, joined the family in 1473. In 1475, a second son, Giovanni, joined the growing brood followed by daughters Luigia and Contessina in 1478 and another son, Giuliano, in 1479.

The majority of the children's care was left to Clarice, though Lorenzo insisted on being kept informed of their routine and academic achievements. He cared deeply for his children and often regretted having to spend so much time away from them. He certainly had a hand in shaping the curriculum that his children studied – as with any children from an upper-class family they learned Greek and Latin from an early age and all desperately wanted to please their father. By the time Piero was 6, he was writing letters to his father in which he said he could not write well at that moment but would do his best, before going on to explain all of the complicated things he'd learned. He certainly comes across as a precocious little boy!

The tutor Lorenzo chose for his children was the poet and scholar Angelo Poliziano. He was a brilliant man who accepted the job as it came hand in hand with friendship of the great Lorenzo the Magnificent, though there were times when he wished for something more. He wanted to work alongside the ruler of Florence, and teaching his children was not exactly what he had in mind. Nevertheless, it brought him closer to the family. Like their father, Lorenzo's children were lively and fun-loving characters. Poliziano wrote to his master in 1479 while staying in the Medici villa of Cafaggiolo, bemoaning the fact that the children were practically running riot: 'The children play about more than usual and are quite restored in health .... I would have liked to serve you in some greater thing, but since this has fallen to my lot, I will do it gladly.'[1]

Unfortunately for the poet, he managed to get on the wrong side of Clarice when it came to the education of the children. The two fell out over what the children should be taught – Clarice decided the Humanist material Poliziano was teaching them was abominable and so, without her husband's consent, had it replaced with more religious texts. In her mind, traditional Christian values were far more important than learning from texts she considered to be pagan and immoral. Poliziano wrote to his master to complain about the changes she had been making and said he didn't approve. He was then dealt an even harder blow when she banished him and sent him packing off to Careggi – far enough away from her and the children that he would not be a problem. Lorenzo tried desperately to smooth things over but it did not work. He stood by his wife and agreed that Poliziano would no longer tutor their children; however he refused to banish the poet from his circle of friends. Poliziano would be with Lorenzo on his deathbed, before meeting his own sudden death a couple of years later. Ironically, Piero and his siblings would grow up appreciating the Humanist texts that their mother so abhorred.

The eldest Medici was brought up knowing that one day he would take over from his father. But the boy was spoiled and, as he grew into a young man, he started to express an egotistical sense of his own worth. He was haughty, looked down his nose at others, and had to be reminded by his father constantly that he was simply a citizen of Florence, not a prince.

At the age of just 13 years old, Piero was sent to Rome on his first diplomatic mission to the new pope, Innocent VIII. Lorenzo had had a rocky relationship with the previous pope, Sixtus, after the awful events of the Pazzi conspiracy. When Lorenzo had executed Archbishop Salviati for his part in the affair, Sixtus had excommunicated not only Lorenzo, but the entire government – never mind the part the pope had played in the whole conspiracy! His death closed the door on a particularly terrible

Bologna, Italy, where Savonarola entered the Dominican Order. (*Adobe Stock*)

Ponte Vecchio in Florence, where Savonarola is remembered on 23 May with flower petals scattered in the water. (*Adobe Stock*)

Bust of Savonarola in San Marco. (*Author's Own*)

Castello Estense in Ferrara. (*Adobe Stock*)

Convent of San Marco, Ferrara. (*Matthew Bryan*)

Door of Savonarola's cell, the *alberghettino*. (*Author's Own*)

Lorenzo de Medici. (*Wikimedia Commons*)

Line engraving of Girolamo's father, Michele Savonarola, 1688. (*Wellcome*)

The Bargello prison where Savonoarola was held. (*Adobe Stock*)

Ferrara, the city of Savonarola's birth. (*Adobe Stock*)

Library of San Marco where Savonarola and his monks tried to wait out the siege, and the friar delivered his goodbye speech. (*Author's Own*)

Nave inside Santa Maria del Fiore. (*Adobe Stock*)

Illustration of the hanging and
burning of Savonarola in Florence.
(*Wikimedia Commons*)

Palazzo Vecchio. (*Author's Own*)

Palazzo Medici-Riccardi in Florence.
(*Adobe Stock*)

Plaque marking the site of Savonarola's
execution. (*Author's Own*)

Pico della Mirandola, who was instrumental in having Savonarola brought back to Florence. (*Wikimedia Commons*)

Piero de' Medici by Domenico Ghirlandaio (*Wikimedia Commons*)

Plaque marking the entrance to Savonarola's cell in San Marco. (*Matthew Bryan*)

Pope Alexander VI by Cristofano dell' Altissimo. (*Wikimedia Commons*)

Plaque on Savonarola's statue. (*Author's Own*)

Portrait of Savonarola. (*Wikimedia Commons*)

Portrait of Italian artist Michelangelo, who admired Savonarola greatly. (*Wikimedia Commons*)

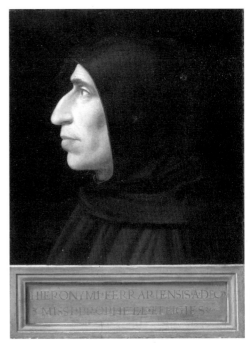

Savonarola by Fra Bartolomeo. (*Wikimedia Commons*)

San Gimignano, where Savonoralo first started preaching. (*Adobe Stock*)

The former Bargello prison is now the art museum, Museo Nazionale del Bargello. (*Adobe Stock*)

Statue of Savonarola outside the Castello Estense, Ferrara. (*Author's Own*)

View of Castello Estense. (*Author's Own*)

Via Savonarola, the street on which Savonarola was born. (*Author's Own*)

View of Santa Maria del Fiore from the tower of the Palazzo Vecchio. Here, Savonarola would preach to the masses. (*Author's Own*)

View from the roof terrace of the Santa Maria del Fiore. (*Author's Own*)

View of the Piazza della Signoria square at sunrise, with Palazzo Vecchio reflected in a puddle. (*Adobe Stock*)

chapter of Lorenzo's life and a new pope meant he could try to rebuild the relationship the Medici once had with the papacy. That was to be the young Piero's job in Rome – a big responsibility for one so young. A letter of instruction was sent with Piero in which Lorenzo reminded his son how important it was to get the pope onside, as well as a reminder to behave and be respectful:

> You will inform His Holiness that I am firmly resolved not to transgress his commands because besides my natural devotion to the Holy See, my devotion to His Beatitude himself arises from many causes and from obligations which ever since I was a child our house has received from him. Add that I have experienced how hurtful it had been to be out of favour with the late pontiff although, as it seems to me, I was unjustly persecuted for other's sins than for any insult or offence to him of holy memory … . Be careful not to take precedence of those who are your elders, for although you are my son, you are but a citizen of Florence.[2]

Alas, his instructions to rein in his bad attitude and high opinions of himself fell on deaf ears. Though his trip to the Eternal City was a success from a business point of view, he returned kitted out in ostentatious clothing which the citizens of Florence did not like one bit.

Lorenzo the Magnificent died on 8 April 1492 – he truly had been magnificent and despite some bumps in the road had been genuinely loved by the citizens of Florence. His passing was mourned deeply and left the city with a feeling of uncertainty as his 20-year-old son stepped up into his place. This feeling of unease grew as Piero began his rule. Piero would prove himself to be beyond incompetent when it came to being in charge.

To start with he did seem to try and follow in his father's footsteps, but lacked the tact and prudence that was undoubtedly required in the tumultuous political world of Renaissance Florence.[3] His character did not lend itself to being head of one of the most powerful families in Italy. He had grown up spoiled, and with a belief that he was better than everyone else. Piero had no tact at all, and when it came to loyalty, he had no idea what the word even meant. He had a violent temper, he was arrogant and lazy, and he was utterly disinterested in politics and the running of the city. When he took the reins of power, he left the day-to-day business to his secretary and had his uncle take control of the now failing Medici bank. He preferred to spend his time outside – one of his better traits was that he was incredibly athletic. It was not long before his reputation was in tatters, not only due to his lack of leadership but because of his haughty wife, Alfonsina Orsini, and his petty arguments with his cousins Lorenzo and Giovanni. These two were from a secondary branch of the Medici family, were considerably richer and older than the young Piero, and they believed that they had more right to be at the top. It was a feud that would last for years.

Following Lorenzo's death, the threat of war loomed over Italy and would, eventually, be a challenge to which Piero de' Medici could not rise. Savonarola, however, took to preaching about this upcoming conflict in earnest, predicting that war and conquest were coming, and this 'prophecy' made the people sit up and take notice. After all, he had correctly prophesied the death of Lorenzo so why should things be any different here? From the pulpit, he boomed that a sword was hanging over Florence, and that a man was coming 'from beyond the mountains like Cyrus, and God shall be his guide and leader, and no one will be able to resist him, and he will take cities and fortresses with great ease.'[4] These words struck fear into his congregation but when, by the beginning of 1493, no Cyrus had made itself known, he began to doubt his own words and for a while refrained from saying anything that could be mistaken for prophecy.

Next, Savonarola began planning on reforming the convent of San Marco. Thanks to his ever-growing popularity and his new way of teaching, the number of novices joining the Dominicans there had risen sharply. In a departure from the stuffy, traditional methods of instruction, he would gather them in the courtyard of the monastery where he would sit beneath a tree and speak to them about the apocalypse. It was far more refreshing for the young novitiates than sitting in a hall and being lectured at.

His popularity, along with the increased fervour of the citizens, meant that the amount of alms collected was now more than enough to support the growing brotherhood. Previously, there had barely been enough money to support the few monks they had and, in an effort to survive, they had joined the Lombard Congregation, a confraternity of Dominican houses who were far from strict when it came to following the vows they had sworn – something that didn't sit comfortably with the friar. Savonarola ensured he and the friars practised what they preached and took their vow of poverty seriously. They were no longer able to own private property, could not own any personal items and their dress became simpler. They may have lived within the walls of a beautiful monastic house, but that did not mean they could live in luxury.

Now, with enough alms to support them, and a group of monks who wished to live pious lives, it was the perfect time to break away. A brief was soon placed before the pope, suggesting that San Marco split from the Lombard congregation and form a separate one, where the brothers would concentrate on living simpler lives not defined by wealth or personal possessions. The brief was approved thanks to the clever machinations of Cardinal Carafa, a friend to the Dominicans and a supporter of Savonarola. As the document was placed before the pope, his Holiness declared that he was far too tired to continue conducting business. Carafa removed the ring from the pope's finger and sealed the brief himself, becoming the one person who allowed Savonarola's plans to move forward and place San Marco directly under the jurisdiction of the Dominican master general. This was the first step to the establishment of a new congregation which had priories at San Marco, Fiesole, Prato and Pisa, and was ruled by Savonarola as vicar general. This allowed him to bring in his wished-for reforms including manual labour for all brothers, to encourage humility, as well as the studies of Hebrew, Syriac and the Chaldean languages. He also introduced longer hours for prayer, plainer items of clothing and water replaced the wine that was served at mealtimes.

Savonarola's warning of a new Cyrus surfaced once again in 1494. Ludovico 'Il Moro' Sforza, ruler of Milan, had become convinced that when Alfonso of Naples succeeded his father, the dangerous King Ferrante, that he would attack. Sforza was particularly paranoid given the fact he had refused to relinquish the regency of Milan once his nephew, Gian Galeazzo, came of age. The young man did not argue with his uncle over this, but rumours began to circulate that he was being poisoned, given just how fragile his health was. Galeazzo's wife, Isabella d'Aragona, went to her grandfather, Ferrante of Naples and begged him to do something about it and help her husband gain what was rightfully his. Despite being known for his love of violence and his treacherous ways, Il Moro – who was given this nickname for two reasons: a pun on Mauro, his middle name, and a reference to the dark and swarthy complexion that many felt made him look Moorish – was understandably worried that by crossing the rulers of Naples, he would end up in serious trouble. When Ferrante died, it started a snowball effect that ended up bringing King Charles VIII to Italy.

Charles believed that he had a solid claim to the throne of Naples and his followers encouraged him to take what was his. After months of dithering, it was agreed that the French Army would invade Italy – they crossed the Alps on 8 September 1494, with the aim of taking control of Naples. This army was massive – 19,000 infantry, 1,900 lances and 1,200 mounted archers, supported by 1,500 Italian lances and around 300 Italian infantry.[5] Finally, Savonarola's new Cyrus was coming, and during his Lenten sermons, he took to the pulpit and cried out: 'Behold, the sword has descended, the scourge has fallen, the prophecies are being fulfilled: behold it is the Lord who is leading on these armies.'[6]

As the French advanced throughout Italy, blood was shed in a way the Italians had never seen before. They were not usually so ferocious on the battlefield and much of the time, battles on Italian soil came away with very few casualties. But in this case the French Army gave no quarter. As it moved southwards, it conquered towns, slaughtering the citizens in their beds while houses were burned to the ground and women were raped.

How could the people of Florence not believe that the friar's prophecies were finally coming true? How could they not be frightened for their very lives? Add in a complete lack of confidence in their leader, Piero, and it made for a particularly explosive situation. And when Savonarola preached that when the French finally arrived, Piero would do the opposite of what he should – and this came true as well – it caused a stir.

As the army advanced through Italy, it met little resistance with many states declaring themselves to be neutral. But to reach Naples, Charles would have to pass through Tuscany, so he sent envoys to Piero seeking permission to pass through Tuscan borders and to publicly back his claim to the throne of Naples. Here, Piero began playing a dangerous game. He kept the envoys waiting for five days and promised full Florentine support to the King of Naples before declaring that Florence would remain completely neutral.

The French king disliked the young Medici immensely after he had sent two disastrous embassies over to France. Florence had always been an ally of the French, so when Piero made the decision to switch his allegiance to Naples, it was seen as a betrayal by Charles and by the Florentines who worked in the French court as ambassadors. One such ambassador, Piero di Gino Capponi, had become a close friend of the French king – a friendship which ended the moment Piero de' Medici made the decision to move his alliance to Naples. He did this without any input from government officials. Even the public knew that and refused to place any blame whatsoever on the Signoria. No, it was all Piero's fault.

His declaration of neutrality angered both sides but France took matters into their own hands – there was absolutely no way they would allow Piero and his city to be neutral. Charles marched on Tuscany anyway.

In an effort to stop the French army, Piero stood up and tried to do the right thing. He hired a number of mercenaries, sent them to key Tuscan fortresses and prepared to take himself off to fight. Unfortunately for him, however, a certain Dominican friar had managed to convince the populace that their doom had come – the sword of the Lord had finally descended. When Piero asked the Signoria for more money to help the city with its defences, they refused. Reeled in by Savonarola, they said that there was no point in defending a city that was already ruined. Piero's cousins agreed and sent a message to the French king offering their full support for him and his invasion, but their message was intercepted and the brothers arrested. They escaped their confinement, however, and managed to find their way to the French encampment where they assured Charles that if Piero were to be got rid of, the city of Florence would readily support French efforts in Naples.

Piero, never a popular leader, realised that he was on his own. No one wanted to help the man in his efforts to protect Tuscany. His next move made him even less popular with the government of the city that he was supposed to lead; without bothering to seek their approval, he left Florence and rode to Charles' camp at Santo Stefano in order to gain his friendship and convince him that he had been wrong in remaining neutral. He offered anything the French king wanted in return for Florence remaining safe from the French forces. Proving himself to have the greater authority, Charles made huge demands of Piero, who acquiesced to every point, handing over Pisa and numerous castles that would have been the last line of Florence's defence, as well as the huge sum of 20,000 florins.[7] The young Medici left believing his mission had been a success as he had done the best he could do to protect his city .

Savonarola, meanwhile, had been on his own excursion to meet the French king and his was much more successful. It took him to Pisa where he was warmly welcomed. The friar spoke to Charles of Church reform and of calling a council to depose Alexander VI – but he also gained firm assurance from the king that, while the French would advance into the city in a triumphal procession, the army was not hostile to Florence or her people. Girolamo Savonarola returned to Florence in good spirits.

However, soon after, his mood changed when his good friend, Giovanni Pico della Mirandola, died aged just 32. Prior to his death, the two men had been collaborating on a piece of work which aimed to fight the influence of astrology – it would become Savonarola's *Treatise against Astrology*. Before his sickness and sudden death, Mirandola had often spoken to his nephew, Gianfrancesco, and said that he would walk barefoot into the world to preach the Gospel. As Pico lay on his deathbed, he was finally inducted into the Dominican Order, despite previously resisting Savonarola's attempts to have him join. This young man, thought of as a genius from an early age and celebrated across Italy for his intelligence, was buried in the Church of San Marco dressed in a Dominican robe.[8] Savonarola mentioned his friend at the end of a sermon just a week later:

> I want to reveal a secret to you which I haven't wanted to tell until now because I wasn't as certain of it as I have been for the last ten hours. I believe all of you knew Count Giovanni of Mirandola who died a few days ago. I want to tell you that on account of the prayers of the friars and some of the good works he did, as well as other prayers, his soul is in purgatory. Pray for him. He came to religion later in life than had been hoped, and therefore he is in purgatory.[9]

Purgatory, then, for a man who had come to religion later in life than Savonarola had hoped. Was this Savonarola wishing that his friend, whose youth had been spent keeping mistresses and making the pope believe he was heretic, had managed to avoid the flames of Hell? Mirandola had kept a mistress until the end of his life, which Savonarola would have known. Was Savonarola admitting then that Pico, like almost everyone else, was a sinner and would end up in purgatory? If a dear friend of the prophet could not bypass purgatory, then neither could anyone else. Many meanings could be deciphered from these words, but perhaps the greatest meaning is that of grief, and a relief that Giovanni Pico della Mirandola would not suffer the torments of Hell.

It seems strange that a young man who, in his youth, dressed ostentatiously and studied Humanism could become such good friends with a friar who lived so simply. Yet become friends they did. Mirandola, despite his rich upbringing, was ready to learn from the Church – he studied Christianity intensely along with other religions, his natural curiosity allowing him to take in religious information like a sponge soaking up water. Savonarola, meanwhile, was deeply religious, almost a zealot. But he too was gifted with great intelligence. Despite their outward differences, Giovanni Pico della Mirandola and Girolamo Savonarola were, perhaps, more similar than many have previously thought. Indeed, they developed a long-lasting friendship that transcended the bounds of difference and perhaps in some way showed the man who would become both prophet and Florence's greatest heretic to be nothing more than human.

Mirandola's body was recently exhumed from its resting place in San Marco and studied in an effort to find out what had ended his life. Scientists found a high concentration of arsenic in the bones and concluded that he, along with Angelo Poliziano whose body was also exhumed, had been poisoned.

Away from Savonarola's personal grief, the conflict rumbled on. When Piero returned to Florence, he was greeted with hostility. The Signoria had not been informed of his decision to visit the king and they were furious. When he tried to go to the Palazzo della Signoria to report to the government, he found the doors locked and he was refused access. The traitorous Piero de' Medici was no longer welcome in the city and the people blamed him for everything that had happened since the French invasion. It mattered little to them that their young leader had believed he was doing his best for Florence – they wanted a scapegoat and were in the grip of hysteria. As he and his men waited in the piazza before the imposing palazzo, the Signoria ordered that the *vacca* be tolled. As it rang out, the citizens were whipped into an almost riotous state, jeering insults at the small party and forcing them back to the safety of the Palazzo Medici. Even with Piero and his comrades hidden away, the people still cried out that he was a traitor to the republic and demanded retribution.

Cardinal Giovanni de' Medici, Piero's younger brother, tried desperately to bring the situation back under control. While the head of the family hid himself away within the walls of his palatial home, the young cardinal gathered up his men and rode around the streets shouting the famous Medici rallying cry of '*Palle!*' ('Balls', which refers to the balls, said to be coins, that are on the Medici crest). The people, though, did not listen. Instead they came back at the cleric with '*Popolo e Libertá!*' ('People and Freedom!')[10] Even those who had once been close to the family joined in with those shouting for their removal, a way of trying to keep themselves safe in the chaos that was unfolding. This is because individuals such as Bernardo del Neri and Niccolò Ridolfi were known supporters of the Medici clan and were no longer welcome in the city.[11]

It had become clear to Piero that he and his family no longer had a place in Florence. He gathered up as many of the family's valuables as he could and took them for safe keeping at San Marco. This was, of course, the home of Savonarola and his Dominican brothers, but it had traditionally been a safe house for the Medici during times of trouble. While many within those monastic walls were loyal to Savonarola and against the family, there were those who were still friends with the Medici clan and vowed to keep the valuables safe. On 9 November 1494, under the cover of darkness, Piero made his way back to Rome.[12] The very next day, he was formally banished from Florence and a price was placed upon his head.

Piero de' Medici, known to history as 'the unfortunate' never returned to Florence. The closest he got was when he took a small force of soldiers to Porta Romano with the aim of taking back his home. But the Florentine people had no intention of letting this poor excuse of a 'leader' back in, so he and his men slunk away. He remained in Italy for the most part, working as if he were a mercenary and selling his sword to the highest bidder. At one point he even worked with the ruthless Cesare Borgia before once again offering his services to the French who promised him – albeit vaguely – that they would help him take back the city of his birth.

It was during his time with the French Army that Piero de' Medici died. In December 1503, the French were defeated by a Spanish force under the command of Gonsalvo de' Cordoba. Yet rather than dying heroically on the battlefield, he lost his life while trying to escape. He drowned in the Garigliano River when his boat capsized.

It was an unfortunate and cowardly end for a man who had led such an unfortunate life. He never saw his family return to their home, nor the ascension of some of his family members to the highest office in the Church, and he would be remembered in history as a man who barely deserved the title of head of the great Medici family. The Medici, longtime princes of the Florentine Republic, had fallen from grace in a fashion that can only be described as dramatic. They were now personae non gratae, and the city that had once been their home now belonged to the imposing, black-robed figure of Girolamo Savonarola.

# Chapter 7

# The Borgia Pope

Florence did not just lose its leader when Lorenzo the Magnificent died in 1492; it was a pivotal year for the country as a whole. Upon the death of Pope Innocent VIII on 25 July the same year, a conclave was called in Rome that would see the election of a man who would go on to become one of the most maligned popes of all time, as well as a particular enemy of Savonarola. Rodrigo Borgia was born on 1 January 1431, in the little town in Jatvia in Valencia, Spain, to Jofré Lanzol I Escriva and his wife Isabel de Borja y Cavanilles, the younger sister of Pope Callixtus III. His parents were cousins, such marriages being relatively common at the time. After his father died when Rodrigo was 6 years old, his uncle, Alonso de Borja, who would later become Pope Callixtus III, took a keen interest in the upbringing and education of his nephew and began to push the little boy towards a career in the Church. He was given Church benefices at an early age, including posts in his hometown as well as Barcelona and Valencia. These opened a door for the young Rodrigo (he did not adopt his mother's family name of Borgia – the Italian version of Borja – until after the elevation of his uncle, Alonso de Borja) that would eventually lead to him being elected to the most powerful position in the Catholic Church.

When Rodrigo was 18, he travelled to Italy where he completed his university education. By rights he should have lost all income from his Spanish benefices when he left the country; however his uncle, now a cardinal, had a word with Pope Nicholas V who issued a papal bull allowing the young man to keep his income. Bologna was the chosen destination for Rodrigo to study canon law; the university had previously welcomed many renowned students, including the poets Dante and Petrarch. After he left, the university became home to the Humanist Erasmus as well as the astronomer Copernicus and the physician Paracelsus.

During his time at university, Rodrigo became well known for his vices and, in particular, his love of women, which was reciprocated eagerly. A contemporary of Rodrigo, Gaspare da Verona, said of the young churchman: '[Rodrigo] is handsome, of a pleasant and cheerful countenance … with a single glance he can fascinate women and attract them to himself more strongly than a magnet draws iron.'[1]

In 1455, Alonso de Borja was elected to the papacy and took the name of Callixtus III. As was usual upon a papal election, he began handing out important roles to his relatives. His nephew, Pedro Luis, was made gonfalonier of the papal armies while Rodrigo was appointed to the cardinalate. Rodrigo was later raised to the post of Vice Chancellor to the Holy See, effectively becoming Callixtus' second in command. He was given this post not only because he was a relative of the pope, but because of his excellent work while away in Ancona, where he was tasked with the mission of bringing the papal territory back into line after its people had revolted and overthrown papal rule. He led a force of troops towards the city and, on the way, threatened to lay siege to the town of Ascoli. It surrendered at once and Rodrigo Borgia was triumphant without a single drop of blood being spilled. It was testament to his intelligence and political acumen, as well as a true ability in negotiation. The situation could certainly have gone very differently.

The post of vice chancellor came with excellent benefits. Not only was Rodrigo right at the top of the chain of command, it it also came with a handsome income – 6,000 ducats per annum. He knew he needed to keep his hands on this position and the power it gave him, and he would remain as vice chancellor until he was elected to the papacy in 1492. Using his wit and charm, Rodrigo Borgia became a popular member of the College of Cardinals and made himself friends who would help him retain his power.

But when Callixtus III died on Sunday, 6 August 1458, Rodrigo found himself in a dangerous situation. Despite his good work, which included his efforts to stop the Ottoman menace from invading the Christian world, Callixtus had been universally hated by the Italians – mainly for being Spanish – and his fellow Spaniards in the papal court fled in fear of their lives. It was evident that any Spaniard in the city would find their lives at risk and rioting was expected. Rodrigo, however, stayed right where he was, and during this time he would prove his political acumen, initially during the conclave that followed his uncle's death. It was generally agreed that no one wanted another foreigner as pope, yet the cardinals locked within the walls of the Vatican could not make up their minds on who to appoint. Cardinal Piccolomini had nine votes, while the French Cardinal d'Estouteville also had nine. It was Rodrigo who broke the stalemate, declaring that he gave his vote to Piccolomini, Cardinal of Siena. It did not take long for every single cardinal within the room to declare that they too stood with the Cardinal of Siena and wanted him to be elected as Pope.[2] Piccolomini was duly elected and took the name of Pius II. This was a clever move by Rodrigo as it stood him in good stead with the new pope, allowing him to keep his powerful post of vice chancellor. He would retain this post during the reigns of a further three popes – it was a career to be proud of and one that gained him a vast amount of wealth. It also allowed him access to an incredible number of women, women who seemed to fall over themselves just to get at the handsome young vice chancellor. Throughout his life, Rodrigo had multiple mistresses who would bear him a number of children. This was nothing new. It was not uncommon for cardinals to openly flout their vows of chastity.

However, Rodrigo did absolutely nothing to keep his private life private. During a trip to Siena in 1459, the women of the town fell under the spell of the handsome young Borgia and he became involved in some rather racy, and public, escapades. When Pius heard of this, he sent him a stern letter, which said:

We are told that the dances were immodest and the seductions of love beyond bounds and that you yourself behaved as if you were one of the most vulgar young men of the age. In truth, I should blush as to set down in detail all I have been told of what happened. Not only these things themselves, but the mere mention of them, are a dishonour to the office you hold.[3]

The letter did not stop there, with Pius admonishing him for bringing his position into disrepute:

They say that in Siena at the moment you are the laughing stock of the city … . It gives a pretext to those who accuse us of using our wealth and our high office in order to indulge in orgies. We are more angry than we can say … . We leave it to your judgement to say if this befits your high office.[4]

Rodrigo wrote back to Pius, telling the pontiff that the whole thing was spurious rumour and lies – which sounds unlikely given his hedonistic reputation and love of women. Pius, however, appeared to take his word for it and replied: 'We have received your letter and take note of the explanation which you give. What you have done, beloved son, is not without blame, even if it is perhaps less grave than I was at first led to believe.'[5]

It is not clear who had the truth of the matter here. Had Pius been told tall tales about Cardinal Borgia, or was Rodrigo twisting the truth to get himself out of trouble? Either way, the vice chancellor would continue to make a name for himself as a man who loved nothing more than spending time with beautiful women.

It was this love of the fairer sex that had him fathering a number of illegitimate children. This was not an unusual situation in the Church – despite taking a vow of chastity, many cardinals and popes had children and used their wealth and power to set their progeny up for life. What was unusual for Rodrigo was that, as well as fathering many illegitimate children, he acknowledged some as legitimate Borgia heirs.

Rodrigo sired his four best known offspring with his favoured mistress, the married Vannozza Cattanei. These children – Cesare, Juan, Lucrezia and Gioffre – would become the cornerstone of the Borgia legend. At some point between September 1475 and April 1476, Vannozza gave birth to a little boy who would go down in history as one of its greatest warlords, and who would be slanderously accused of activities – including incest – that would be linked with his name for centuries after his death. It was obvious that the child was not fathered by Vannozza's husband – she had been Rodrigo's mistress for at least two years before the birth of the child – and he was given the name Cesare. After Cesare, she gave birth to three more children whose paternity was attributed to Rodrigo Borgia – Juan, often seen as his favourite son, was born in 1476; Lucrezia in 1480 and Gioffre in 1481. Rodrigo was of the belief, however, that Gioffre could not be his child as his relationship with Vannozza had long since cooled off. She maintained that Gioffre was his and again, in another unusual move, to please his former mistress and mother of his adored children, he took Gioffre in and considered him to be his son.

Rodrigo had big plans for these children and from an early age it was decided that they would be used as pawns on his political chessboard; a way of cementing an incredibly powerful dynasty. Juan was to be the military man while Cesare was to be a prince of the Church, perhaps rising high enough to one day become Pope. Lucrezia would be married into a powerful dynastic family. The children were brought up away from their mother, and in their own households, as befitted children of a cardinal. Education was very important and Cesare was given an excellent university education where he studied canon law, attending both the universities of Perugia and Pisa, where the young cleric was praised for his 'ardent mind'.[6]

When Innocent VIII died, in July 1492, he had been pope for eight years, and had succeeded Sixtus IV in the papal conclave that had been Rodrigo Borgia's first real attempt at winning the throne of St Peter. This time, however, it would be more than an attempt on Borgia's part. It would also see an attempt by Giuliano della Rovere to become pope – and a full-blown breakdown in relations between the two men. As Innocent lay on his deathbed, the two men fought by his side, and quarrelled publicly over who would be given the keys to the fortress of the Castel Sant'Angelo.

On 6 August 1492, less than a fortnight after Innocent's death, Rodrigo Borgia entered the conclave. He would prove himself to be very wily and by the time he stepped out of those walls he would have acceded to the highest position in the Catholic Church.

The cardinals who were locked inside were already split into two main factions. One supported the favourite to win – Cardinal Giuliano della Rovere, nephew of Sixtus IV, and preferred choice of the king of France – while the other supported Ascanio Sforza, a member of the famous ruling family of Milan. This split meant that there would be a deadlock and no outright winner could be chosen, so the wheeling and dealing began in earnest. It was rumoured that before the conclave had even begun, the French king had transferred 200,000 ducats to Rome to ensure della Rovere's election. The king's wish, however, would not come true; at this point, della Rovere had absolutely no chance at becoming pope and French interference was not welcome.

During the first week, no one came out with any sort of majority in the voting. This was when Borgia started to show his hand, proving that he was very willing to bribe people for what he wanted. Borgia was not only intelligent, he had an astute political mind – this was a man who had, after all, held on to the post of Vice Chancellor to the Holy See for many years. He even managed to turn Ascanio Sforza to his cause by promising Sforza the post of vice chancellor as well as a vast amount of cash. The story goes that a number of mules were seen carrying cases of gold and silver to Sforza's palazzo in payment for his vote.[7] It is likely, however, that this was made up by Stefano Infessura, an early biographer of Pope Alexander VI, who was anti-pope and anti-Borgia in particular. We are able to gauge this because he stated that Borgia gave his house to Cardinal Orsini as a reward for voting his way, when the house was actually given to Sforza. The Borgia myth also claims that Rodrigo promised benefices to the cardinals who voted for him, but the more likely explanation is that they were given to the three biggest Roman families simply to keep the peace. For example, the castles of Soriano and Castellana, and the Abbey of Subiaco, were given to cardinals Orsini, Colonna and Savelli.[8] Of course, enemies of the Borgia family would start the rumour mill that simony, bribery and corruption were rife in Rodrigo's bid for power, and perhaps they were, but it has to be said that he was fair. He rewarded every cardinal following his election to the papacy – even those who stood against him got something out of the new pope. Della Rovere, for instance, was given the Abbey of Rioux and a pension of fifty ducats per year.

By the fourth day of the election, Rodrigo Borgia was so close to winning the papacy he could practically taste it. He had done his utmost to wheel and deal his way through the cardinals who stood in his way, but a few still stood firm. They would never vote for another Spaniard, and certainly not a Borgia. His final hope lay in the aged Cardinal Maffeo Gheradi. Borgia swayed the 86-year-old Venetian and on the fifth day of the conclave, 11 August 1492, Rodrigo Borgia's name was announced as having the required majority.

Borgia, who stood up on hearing news and shouted, 'I am Pope!', took the name of Alexander VI as homage to Alexander the Great. He wanted to build an empire just as Alexander had done, and this name was the first step in his dynastic plans. He was generally greeted favourably by the Christian world although, of course, there were some who started whispering about how Borgia had bought his way to the chair of St Peter. He threw himself into the role with gusto, proving himself to be far cleverer than anyone could have imagined. He was ruthless too.

Obviously, Borgia's ungodly behaviour – a religious man who had taken a vow of chastity but was proud of his numerous children – caught the attention of the puritanical Savonarola, who already had issue with the corruption of the Church. The begetting of children and the sin of nepotism were not the only issues that would have caused Savonarola's anger – it was also the rumour that Borgia had committed the sin of simony, or the buying and selling of ecclesiastical offices, in order to gain the throne of St Peter. It was the kind of conduct that Savonarola hoped to stamp out and spent much of his time attacking in his sermons. They were never going to see eye to eye, but Girolamo Savonarola made the mistake of crossing this ruthless Spaniard; a man who had no qualms in ordering the deaths of those who stood against him. And it would prove to be the biggest mistake the friar would ever make.

# Chapter 8

# A Duel of Religious Giants

Savonarola underestimated Pope Alexander VI from the start. According to the friar, there was no way a man as corrupt as Rodrigo Borgia could be pope and he had no qualms in preaching as much to his followers. Although he never spoke the Borgia pope's name in his sermon, it was obvious about whom he was speaking. Alexander was fully aware of everything that was being said and he was angry. He sent a barrage of letters to Florence, demanding that the Dominican cease preaching such views and asking him why he was encouraging division and conflict with his prophecies when he claimed to be such a Godly person. Despite his anger, his letters were relatively polite, as this extract shows:

> You ought to have preached unity and peace, instead of these things which the populace calls prophecies and divinations … for if by their own nature they are liable to cause discord even if complete peace were reigning.[1]

The Pope's warning was clear, but the letters were met with scorn, and each one was ignored. In fact, Savonarola continued to preach until July 1495, when he secluded himself in the Tuscan countryside to recover his health. Evidently, leading the people of Florence and preaching constantly in front of thousands of people was too much for him and his health was suffering. But taking a holiday from spouting his grievances was not enough for Pope Alexander – he wanted to bring the outspoken friar to heel and he had what he thought was the perfect weapon to attack. On 8 September 1495, a papal brief arrived in Florence. This document was not actually written by the Pope but rather the Bishop of Cosenza and papal secretary Bartolomeo Floridi. Nevertheless, it would still carry significant weight in Florence. In a clever move, the brief was not delivered directly to Savonarola at San Marco, but, perhaps deliberately in order to make sure that word spread quicker, to the rival monastery of Santa Croce. Residents of this monastery harboured some of the most anti-Savonarolan feelings within the city. As expected, news of the brief spread like wildfire and had crossed the town before it was even delivered to San Marco. Everyone knew but Savonarola, who was still out of the city.

The document mentioned Savonarola by name and dissolved the independent Tuscan Congregatio, forcing it to move back into the Congregation of Lombardy. These congregations were groups of religious houses and cities, which were run similarly to church parishes today. It was made very clear that the united congregations would be headed by Sebastiano Magi, the vicar general of the Lombardy Congregation. Magi would, in turn, conduct an investigation into Savonarola and his anti-papal preaching. The brief finished with a very clear statement – Girolamo Savonarola was suspended from all forms of preaching.[2] Ignoring anything that was in the brief would lead to instant excommunication, not only for the wayward friar, but the entire population of Florence, a rare papal move known as an interdict. Yet another nail was driven into the coffin when Alexander sent a letter to the governing Signoria of Florence warning that if they continued to support Savonarola and allow him to preach to the masses, they would all face the same punishment. He added, as an extra threat to show he was serious, that he would happily give money to Piero de' Medici to help in the restoration of the Medici family. The Pope certainly was not playing any games. But Savonarola played the pontiff at his own game.

When he finally received the news, he argued in a long letter that he was acting as any humble friar would, and there was no way he was trying to, or would ever try to, take on the Pope. His argument was broken down into clear and systematic points – one asserted that he had never once claimed to be a prophet, while another said that the separation of the Tuscan and Lombard Congregations was nothing to do with him, but rather Cardinal Carafa.[3]

Savonarola was then to make his first mistake. Evidently satisfied with himself, he decided to go against the orders in the papal brief and carry on preaching. The friar even told his supporters – who had heard a rumour that Piero de' Medici was planning a coup in order to get his family back in power – that he and the Pope had come to an agreement . Standing before his congregation he roared that they should have absolutely no qualms about putting anyone to death who tried to bring despotism and tyranny back to the city of Florence.[4] This move, a bold yet stupid one on Savonarola's part, culminated in his being sent another letter. This one ordered the friar to stop preaching indefinitely, until he could present himself before Alexander in Rome.

The silence did not last long, however. In 1496, Pope Alexander made a rare political mistake. He realised that enforcing silence upon the outspoken churchman would upset Charles VIII, a Savonarola supporter whom the Pope desperately wanted as his ally. Alexander could very easily have finished the friar with an excommunication, but he held back, and this allowed Savonarola to return to the pulpit where he once more spoke vehemently about Church reforms and the corruption of the pope. As always, these sermons were full of ominous apocalyptic images, but this time he stated unequivocally that the Pope was simply a man and that the people of Rome should not be taking any sort of religious orders from him.

It was somewhat akin to the teachings of the Bohemian heretic Jan Hus, who was arrested and executed during the Council of Constance in 1415. In some senses, Hus was both a precursor of Savonarola and of the Reformation of the sixteenth century. Dean and rector of Prague University in Bohemia (now Czechoslovakia) he opposed the Catholic church on moral and philosophical grounds. In particular, he challenged orthodox views on the eucharist, with its concept of the wine and bread of the communion element of the Mass *becoming* the blood and flesh of Christ. But it was his attack on the corruption of the Church that captured the imagination and which gave hm a link with the Florentine friar at the heart of this book.

Like Savonarola, Hus's early years showed no sign of the radical, the reformer. In Hus's time (he was born about 1372) there was not even the notion of Humanism to colour his early acceptance of Church philosophy. By the time he was teaching and delivering sermons in Prague, however, he railed particularly against simony, the way in which the Church, spearheaded by Rome, made money out of the flock. As he himself put it, 'the very last penny which an old woman has hidden in her bundle for fear of thieves ... will not be saved. The villainous priest will grab it.'

Hus was not talking about criminous clerks, the group of bent clergy who used their position to extort and manipulate the laity. He meant that the Church was institutionally corrupt, from the humblest priest who cajoled his parishioners into coughing up collections to the pardoner who sold indulgences (get out of Hell free cards) to the pope who not only tolerated all this, but often had a wife, mistress and children in a role that was supposed to be celibate.

Hus's career is very like that of Savonarola. Both men were insiders, clerks in holy orders who knew, sometimes literally, where the bodies were buried. The Bohemian's sermons eventually reached the ears of the pope, Alexander V, and he was promptly excommunicated. Like Savonarola, Hus was popular – anybody was who exposed tyranny – and he had a huge following. The result was that the bull of excommunication was not enforced and Hus continued to spout his radical rhetoric from the pulpit. Worse, arguably, he was teaching heresy to susceptible young minds at the university.

Just as Savonarola was invited several times to go to Rome to defend himself, Hus was invited to the Council of Constance in 1414, a fatal move as it turned out. Constance was one of those seminal conferences of the Middle Ages at which the Church took a firm stand against dissent by labelling it all heresy. It would have been sensible for Jan Hus to decline the offer, but, in his own words again, 'I would not, for a chapel of gold, retreat from the truth'. He effectively signed his own death warrant with this stance and he was burned for heresy on 6 July 1415. As the flames spat upwards from the faggots, he could be heard singing psalms in his agony.

As with Martin Luther and other leaders of the Reformation, indeed, with Savonarola himself, later generations hijacked Hus for their own ends. The Hussites, led by their formidable mercenary general, Jan Ziska, formed an army and fought countless skirmishes in Bohemia in the years 1420–31. They forgot, if they ever understood, Hus's philosophical nuances. To the Hussites, the corrupt Catholic Church was the enemy and Hus himself a martyr who must be avenged.

Where did Jan Hus's ideas come from? By the late fourteenth century, many thinking men (and the few women who were allowed to think!) realized that the church of which they were a part was irredeemably corrupt. But it took a brave man to say so and arguably, the first of these was the Englishman John Wycliffe. Like Hus, a cleric and scholar, Wycliffe was teaching at a university – Oxford – in the 1360s and advocated (although he did not undertake it himself) the translation of the Latin Bible into English. Most ordinary Englishmen at the time spoke no Latin at all, so that the priests *hoc est corpus* (this is the body) at the Communion Mass became hocus pocus (nonsense) to them. Wycliffe also attacked the stultifying rigidity of the Church its views on monasticism, predestination and the papacy. Above all, in keeping with most of the radicals of the sixteenth century Reformation, he believed in a strict return to the Gospels. Anything else was later church doctrine and should be treated warily.

His supporters were not as militant as Huss but the Lollards (from the Dutch word for mumblers) took up the cause after Wycliffe's death in 1384. The mini-rebellion led by Oldcastle against Henry V on the eve of Agincourt was Lollard-inspired. Geoffrey Chaucer, though far too clever to be obvious in his views, clearly despised the Church. Of the eight churchmen in his Canterbury Tales (c. 1386) only one, the humble parish priest, is a good, honest man. The others have broken virtually every commandment in the book.

Even though Wycliffe escaped the fate of Hus, he too was declared a heretic at the Council of Constance when the Church was in a militant mood to sweep the board of its enemies.

How far Savonarola was influenced, if at all, by Hus and Wycliffe is debatable. We know that Hus had read the works of the Oxford scholar because they were available (in Latin) in Prague by 1399. Savonarola, as an insider, would have been familiar with the decisions made at Constance. The common theme to all three men, although they differed in terms of philosophy and doctrine, was the corruption of the Church as it had evolved by the fourteenth and fifteenth centuries.

The Pope sent a group of men to Florence to investigate Savonarola's sermons after hearing reports that they were heretical. They reported back that Savonarola was not preaching heresy at all. Alexander was running out of ideas and in one last attempt to bring the wayward friar to heel he sent Fra Ludovico, Captain General of the Dominican Order, to Florence to speak to him. The two had a meeting in which Ludovico offered the friar a cardinal's hat if he would acquiesce to the Pope's demands. In true Savonarola style he gave his answer publicly, in a sermon the very next day. As he stood before his congregation in the Great Hall of the Palazzo della Signoria he turned the offer down:

> People are saying that the Frate wants money, the Frate has secret dealings, the Frate would like a cardinal's hat. Well, I can tell everybody that if I coveted such things, I wouldn't be wearing a ragged habit. I just want to be glorified in You, my God. I don't have any desire for a hat or for a mitre, whether it's a big one or a little one, but only for the gift that you give to your saints – death, a crimson hat, a hat of blood, that's what I want.[5]

In May 1497, Pope Alexander VI excommunicated Girolamo Savonarola. His efforts to get him to stop preaching had been ignored and his offer of a cardinal's hat was all but laughed at, so he felt that he had no other choice. The brief of excommunication was received a month later, at a time when opposition towards the friar was starting to ramp up. Unrest was building in Florence and Savonarola's reliance on Charles VIII of France was starting to be a problem. Additionally, the Signoria were becoming pro-Medici again with the election as gonfalonier of Bernardo del Nero, a staunch supporter of the Medicean regime. And then, to add fuel to the fire, just a few days before the excommunication came into force, the pulpit in the Santa Maria del Fiore was coated in dirt and excrement.[6] Perhaps the people of Florence were showing Savonarola what they really thought of the words coming out of his mouth.

Savonarola's popularity was diminishing. After all, the excommunication, and his response to it, affected the people of Florence as well as the wayward friar, and the Signoria were growing more wary of him and his sermons. Despite arguing that he had never said such a thing, he had indeed called himself a prophet – and while he had predicted the coming of a new Cyrus, it had not ended as he had hoped. The people were starting to miss the way things had been under the rule of the Medici – Savonarolan Florence was not fun; art and gambling were frowned upon; Carnevale had been turned into a religious festival and the people were getting disgruntled.

Stunned by the excommunication, Savonarola stopped preaching for a while and kept to himself. It was during this time that he wrote *The Triumph of the Cross*, which was an investigation into the workings of the Christian faith.

This is probably one of Savonarola's most famous works and discusses the differences between outer and inner worship. According to him, a Christian should aspire to inner peace; an odd claim considering his reliance on outward preaching. In the work he writes: 'It is evident that perfection of life is a more true religion than any exterior form of worship.'[7]

According to Savonarola, inner peace allows martyrs to face their death without any sort of fear. Is it possible that when he faced his own death, he remembered on his own words?

In essence, this book was written by Savonarola as an antidote to the accusations of heresy levelled at him and to put forward his true feelings towards the Church. *The Triumph of the Cross* is split into four books – the first documents the existence and nature of God, and aims to prove the immortality of the soul of man; the second aims to show how the Christian faith works alongside truth and reason; the third attempts to explain that nothing is impossible within the Christian faith, and the fourth goes into detail about the truth of the religion that was taught by Jesus Christ. The entire work was written to show how those opposed to the Christian faith (astrologers, Jews and heretics are just a few of the examples given) were completely and utterly at odds with to reason.[8] And it expressed how devoted Savonarola was to the Church and its teaching. However, it did little to change the minds of his detractors.

His silence did not last for long and, with his book complete, he was soon back in his pulpit openly flouting the excommunication. Alexander was apoplectic and decided that he would now eliminate the outspoken and overly stubborn friar once and for all. As Savonarola continued to preach, the Pope sent letter after letter to the Signoria demanding that the friar be handed over or imprisoned in Florence until he was ready to go to Rome and submit himself to the Pope's rule. The letters also said that if the Signoria refused to do this then they, and the entire city, would be placed under an interdict – which would mean the people of Florence would not be allowed to take part in any official Church activities, including funerals. Any individual who died during this time would not be allowed last rites, and thus would be damned to Hell in the eyes of the Church.

As usual, the Signoria were split when they met to work out what to do with Savonarola. Some believed he should be handed over to the Pope to face the consequences of his outspoken and probably heretical actions while others thought he should be allowed to carry on. Eventually they came to an agreement – Girolamo Savonarola would have to stop preaching, but he would not be handed over to the Pope.[9]

The friar took heed, but he found a loophole and was still openly flouting the Pope's excommunication and the Signoria's decision. He had other Dominican friars preach in his stead and speak out against the excommunication. Then he went one step further. He wrote letters to some of the most powerful rulers in the world – the Holy Roman Emperor, Maximilian I and the kings of France, England and Spain – and asked them to summon a general council of the Church. It was his aim that this council would end in the deposition of his bitter enemy, Alexander VI. There was just one problem. The letters were delivered straight into the hands of the Pope rather than to their intended recipients.[10]

The duel between these two religious giants was about to come to a head. Neither wished to back down and they were as stubborn as each other, but one was the head of the Church of Rome and one of the most powerful men in the world while the other was a lowly friar who simply had a way with words. They were about to lock horns in a battle that would end in a trial by fire, torture and a brutal execution. Girolamo Savonarola was on a fast-paced downward spiral from which he would not return.

# Chapter 9

# The Bonfire of the Vanities

T he term 'Bonfire of the Vanities' causes anyone with an interest in art history to recoil in horror at the very thought of the great works of art that went up in flames. Between Lent of 1497 and 1498 many hundreds of paintings – works of art and books by some of the greatest artists and writers in history – were consigned to the fire because they were seen as ungodly, and it was believed by Savonarola and his followers that they inspired ungodly thoughts. In his infinite wisdom, Savonarola decided to hold these bonfires as a way of boosting morale in Florence during an already worrying political climate. War was, as ever, brewing and some of the most powerful individuals in Italy were trying to get rid of the friar before he could manage to bring Charles VIII back into the country. One of these individuals was the ruler of Milan, Ludovico 'Il Moro' Sforza. He summoned both the Ferrarese and Florentine envoys to an audience with him and presented them with two letters – both apparently written by the infamous Dominican friar – about which the Duke was absolutely furious. These letters, which were obviously forgeries, had apparently been found en route to the French Court addressed personally to Charles VIII. One of them urged the French king to invade Italy as soon as was humanly possible. Il Moro was so angry that he immediately sent copies of the letter to every head of state and kingdom in Italy. Despite the fact that these were obvious fakes, Savonarola was worried and made a public announcement in which he denied having anything to do with them.

Despite his claims, the outcome was as expected – dislike of Savonarola kept on growing and his enemies multiplied. When Il Moro decided to involve the Holy Roman Emperor in his plans to thwart an apparently advancing Charles, it only made matters worse for Florence. Money was supplied by Venice and the Pope, and the Emperor marched on Italy and took control of the city of Livorno, which was seen as the gateway to Florence. A Venetian fleet blockaded the port while the Emperor and a group of Pisan soldiers attacked from land. This brilliantly tactical move left Florence entirely on its own – Charles VIII even wrote to Savonarola to say that he had absolutely no plans to come back to Italy.[1]

In another blow to Savonarola, Piero de' Medici was heavily involved in the intrigue plans between Il Moro and the Holy Roman Emperor. The young Medici and his allies had already gained confidence thanks to the election of the pro-Medicean Bernardo del Nero as gonfalonier and had been making their own plans to move on Florence. Pisa was a key city in this fight, and everyone wanted control of it, so when the Emperor decided he did too, it both the Venetians and the Milanese. Piero was clear, however, that Pisa should remain Florentine territory and this would be lost unless he took control.[2] Despite the fall out between the Emperor, Milan, Venice and Piero, Florence was still totally cut off. There was only the faintest glimmer of hope when, on 16 November 1496, a huge gale caused the Venetian admiral's ships to sink, cutting off the allies from their naval comrades. However, this victory, which was probably seen by Savonarola and his followers as a sign from God that they would triumph, was short-lived. This war was taking up vast amounts of resources which led to widespread dissent within Florence. The price of food shot up so much that families and their children starved. Even when the Signoria handed out free grain to the poor, those within the crowds were suffocated and trampled in the rush to feed themselves. Luca Landucci, the Florentine diarist, reported that he had seen people collapse in the streets, dying from starvation before his very eyes. He wrote: 'More than one child was found dead of hunger in Florence … . During all this time, men, women and children were falling down, exhausted from hunger, and some died of it, and many died at the hospital who had grown weak from starvation.'[3]

Savonarola believed he knew how to boost the morale of the city. He was aware of the abject misery of the people and so organised for Shrove Tuesday – a day when Carnevale is held – to be marked by a special bonfire, much more special than the bonfire that normally marked the religious holiday. This bonfire was so unique that he sent his army of children out into the city to gather up what he called 'vanities'. At his request, his troop of boys went from house to house, knocking on doors and collecting all the items requested, which were handed over willingly. In Savonarola's eyes, a vanity was considered to be an instrument of vice or evil, so the boys collected up paintings showing non-religious scenes or nudity, lewd books, fancy dresses, naked statues, books by classical authors such as Ovid ... the list goes on. Even Sandro Botticelli handed over his own work willingly. Savonarola's sermons had had an effect on him. While the artist continued to include nudity in his paintings, one of his later works, *Mystical Crucifixion*, completed circa 1500, is a gloomy portrait of flames and dark clouds behind a crucifix, while Mary Magdalen lies at the bottom. These images were clearly inspired by Savonarola's messages and prophecies.

The vanities were carried to the Piazza della Signoria where they were piled into a huge pyramid made up of several tiers. Once complete, an image of the devil was placed at the top. Each tier was loaded with different types of vanities and the closer they were to the devil, the more evil they were considered to be. Unsurprisingly, the bonfire was controversial and a Venetian merchant offered the Signoria the huge sum of 20,000 florins to save these items from going up in flames. He was refused.[4]

On the morning of the bonfire, Savonarola celebrated Mass for thousands of people before a procession wound its way towards the Piazza della Signoria. It was led by four of Savonarola's boys, the Fanciulli, who carried a platform between them, on top of which was a statue, carved by Donatello, of the baby Jesus. Draped on this statue was a silk canopy, which was carried by another twelve boys; and they were followed by the rest of the Fanciulli, who walked in twos towards the piazza. Once they arrived, the boys positioned themselves around the edge of the square and sang hymns as the great pyramid was set alight.[5] The growing flames triggered great rejoicing for those crowded within the square to watch the inferno. As the bells of the palazzo rang out, for a brief time the citizens were able to forget their troubles and their hunger and celebrate.

Nearly every item that ended up on the pyramid was handed over willingly. Many artists other than Botticelli surrendered their works, including Lorenzo di Credi and Fra Bartolomeo, who was known as Baccio della Porta until he joined the priory at San Marco. These artists had been inspired by Savonarola to change their ways of working, and their artwork would take on a far more religious form. Della Porta would go on to paint the now well-known portrait of Savonarola with its note at the top stating that it was an image of a 'prophet sent by God'.[6] The painter was so enamoured with Savonarola and his ideas, and so grieved by Savonarola's eventual death, that for a long time afterwards, he stopped creating art.

So why would these artists hand over their work, many of which were masterpieces, without argument? The answer is simple – they had been hooked and reeled in by Savonarola and his rhetoric, awed by his sermons and talk of prophecy and the apocalypse, and they wholeheartedly believed that he could bring about his promised City of God, that he would turn Florence into a new Jerusalem.[7]

He had much support amongst artists. Michelangelo admired the friar greatly and although his admiration lasted for the rest of his life, Michelangelo had escaped the city, having been invited to Rome by Cardinal Riario. It was there, in the corruption and vice of the Holy City, that Michelangelo created his first religious piece of art. It could be said that had he stayed in Florence, the genius he was so well known for would never have been fulfilled.

Despite consigning many beautiful works of art to the flames, Savonarola did not disapprove of art or artists generally, and, as noted, even had his own portrait painted. But he disapproved of art that showed any sort of vice. If a piece of art took away from the message of Christ then it was inappropriate and would not be tolerated in his city, which is precisely why so many nude paintings and statues were burned on the huge pyre. Burning these items so publicly sent that message to the citizens of Florence loud and clear.

But the party atmosphere could not last. People were still going hungry because of the ongoing famine and the dearth of cheap grain.

More shockingly, France had abandoned the Florentines by signing a truce with those who had created the Holy League; a league created by Pope Alexander VI in order to stop the invasion of Charles VIII and his army, involving Spain, the Holy Roman Emperor, Ludovico Sforza and Venice – and were joined by England in 1496. It left the Florentine people isolated and extremely vulnerable to the pressures of the Pope and his league. The truce had scuppered Savonarola and his prophecies. Had not the friar proclaimed that Charles would be a new Cyrus? That Charles would arrive in force to help turn Florence into a new Jerusalem? These questions lingered with those who opposed the friar and they began to get louder, denouncing him once again as a false prophet. In typical Savonarolan fashion, he struck back – except this time it came across as callous and insensitive, making the citizens feel as if he cared little for their hunger and blaming them for their suffering: 'You people lament the famine, but you don't say how much you deserve it because of your sins,' he said. 'God is angry with you; famine is in you and in your hands, because if you do good God will help you in everything.'[8]

Savonarola's star was fading, and his enemies began to gain confidence and visibility. Support for Piero de' Medici, which had often remained hidden, became more explicit and Bernardo del Nero, an ardent Medicean supporter, was voted in as gonfalonier of the Signoria. Not only was a Medicean now in power but it was a snub to the previous gonfalonier Francesco Valori who had supported Savonarola and his methods. Things would be changing with Nero and, slowly but surely, he would chisel away at the world Savonarola had created for the citizens of Florence.

Still, the friar continued to wield his power. When opposition to his rule and reforms came from a nun, Suor Maddalena, who lived at the convent of Santa Maria di Casignano, he managed to have her exiled from Florence. When she was brought to the city in order to confront and embarrass the friar, Savonarola refused to meet her. It would, he argued, give her credibility where absolutely none was due. His adamant refusal brought in a group of officials whose job it was to solve disputes between factions – they came to the conclusion that in order to have peace in Florence, Savonarola should be banished. But the Medicean Signoria, still finding their way in a city that was only just starting to see sense, decided that Maddalena should be the one to go. Savonarola was safe … for now.

He could not have known it, but he was on the precipice. With pro-Mediceans in power, was it any wonder that an emboldened Piero de' Medici decided to march on the city that had once been his home? And march he did, with a small army, but luck was not on his side. Firstly, bad rainfall forced him to turn back and wait for the weather to clear. Once it had, he assembled a bigger army and marched on the walls of Florence again. He shouted his demands, calling for a *parlamento*, but it fell on deaf ears, and he was left waiting for hours until he grew bored and decided to turn back. It was obviously not the right time for the Medici to return to the city; not when Savonarola still held at least some sway over the government. Yet still there was dissent, especially when it came to the friar's preaching, which was not helped with the re-election of the priors in the Signoria who were fervently anti-Savonarola. Another new gonfalonier, Alberti, moved to introduce a two-month ban on unlicensed preaching – a ban that seemed to be aimed directly at Savonarola. Knowing full well he was the target, Savonarola tried to block the vote but he needed five votes and only managed four. He did, however, achieve one small concession – he would be allowed to preach on Ascension Day, something his friends urged him against, as it was whispered that his enemies were planning a demonstration that could turn violent. The friar ignored the advice and when the day came, he preached though the night before a disgusting warning was placed on the pulpit inside the cathedral – the corpse of an ass was nailed up and faeces were smeared across the walls.

It did not stop Savonarola from preaching. He railed against his detractors and the demonstrators still came, but Savonarola made his way back to San Marco, accompanied by many of his supporters, where he continued his Ascension Day sermon.

He was safe within the walls of San Marco, at least for now. He still held influence and the general support of the citizens, but despite his efforts to calm the people with his bonfires and preaching, he was not as revered as he had been previously. The waters were becoming choppy and soon they would sweep Girolamo Savonarola away.

# Chapter 10

# The Tables Turn

For Alexander VI, enough was enough and he began to plan ways to bring about Savonarola's downfall. However, in Florence, they were doing some of the work for him. Support for the Medici was growing once again, especially with new pro-Medicean members of the Signoria being voted in. This had happened due to a mistake made by gonfalonier Francesco Valori, which allowed the Signoria to be flooded with young men who despised Savonarola and wanted the Medici back in power – Valori had lowered the age qualification for the Grand Council from 30 to 24. Not long after, he was ousted from power and a new gonfalonier elected in his place. Bernardo del Nero took the key position in government and, as this was a man who had been a huge supporter of the Medici, the pendulum began to swing in their favour. While he did not have much faith in Piero, he hated Savonarola and the way the government was being run thanks to his influence. The election of del Nero gave the anti-Savonarolan Bigi hope for the restoration of the Medici, and Savonarola was starting to become suspicious that the government were working against him.

In March 1497, Giulio d'Este, the son of the Duke of Ferrara, crept into Florence to hear the friar preach. He was alarmed at what he heard and had the Ferrarese ambassador, Manfredo Manfredi, report to the monastery of San Marco to speak to Savonarola. The friar was appropriately effusive, saying that he was grateful for Ferrara's support. But the next day he gave Manfredi a letter addressed to Ercole d'Este, telling the duke that he was aware of how bad the political situation was getting and that he was doing his best to ensure the peace of the city.

But Savonarola could not give Florence peace and harmony. Rumours abounded that Piero de' Medici was planning to march on the city, and although they were unfounded, it gave rise to more anti-Savonarolan feeling. From Rome, the Pope watched with glee. Things were finally starting to go his way and now he could show his hand – on 12 May 1497, Alexander began to complain loudly that a 'certain friar' was continuing to preach 'pernicious dogma' despite being ordered to stop.[1] These complaints were written down in a breve – or letter of authority from a pope or monarch – and ended by saying that anyone who attended his sermons or had any sort of contact with him was at risk of excommunication. Copies of this breve were sent to all the churches in Florence along with a letter addressed to the Signoria – but when Savonarola heard about it, he wrote to the Pope in order to stave off any sort of excommunication. He wrote that he had been accused of many things, but that it was all false, and he was innocent, and that the one who should be punished was 'that certain and illustrious orator' Fra Mariano.[2] He wrote:

What do I preach, then, with all my strength and the power of my voice but repentance of sin and the mending of our ways, for the sake of Our Lord Jesus Christ, while I labour to revive that faith which is almost extinguished in men's hearts? Soon, by the grace of God, I shall publish a work *De Triumpho Christi* in defence of the faith, from which it will be apparent whether I am a sower of heresies (that may I never be!) or of Catholic truth. I beg Your Holiness, therefore, not to lend faith to the envious and the slanderers, without first having assured yourself of this, as they could already be shown openly to have been guilty of many lies. If human aid should then fail me and the wickedness of the impious prevail, I shall trust in God, my help, and make known their wickedness to the whole world, so that perhaps they will repent once and for all of their undertaking.[3]

This letter did nothing to stop Alexander's plans and, on 18 June 1497, the Order of Excommunication arrived in the city and was read out in five of its most important churches – including Santa Croce, Santa Maria Novella and Santo Spirito – along with the ritual of 'the bell, the book and the candle'. This involved small bells being rung out and two large candles being held upside down, only to have their wicks snuffed out on the ground in an imitation of the excommunicant having been snubbed from the grace of God.[4]

Savonarola reacted by carrying on as if nothing had happened. After all, the breve said that that he was only *suspected* of heresy, and not actually found guilty of that grave crime. There were no formal charges, and so there would be no trial; it was as if this excommunication was a stern warning of what would happen *if* Savonarola kept on causing trouble. But while the friar was not all that bothered, his enemies thought it was the start of something big, and the divisions between the factions only deepened, despite the best efforts of the Signoria to stop the fighting. In March they had summoned the leaders of the factions to the Palazzo della Signoria to sort the whole mess out amicably, but it did not work. The Signoria themselves remained divided over what they should do about the rebellious friar. Did they side with Rome and stop him from preaching, or just let him carry on? They could not decide.

To make a modern comparison with Savonarola's reactions to his enemies, it can be described as Trumpesque. In much the same way as the 45th President of the United States took to social media to condemn the 'witch-hunt' of those who spoke out against him and the 'hoax' of the impeachment proceedings against him and his government, Girolamo Savonarola stood in the pulpit of the cathedral and roared to his congregation that those who stood against him were doing so to tarnish the name of the government, the new Jerusalem of Florence, the word of God *and* he himself, a simple and lowly friar. After all, was not trying to 'Make Florence Great Again'? There are many comparisons that can be made with Trump's presidency, despite the general consensus that the historian should not judge individuals from the past with a modern mindset. In this case, however, that is easier said than done.

Despite his outspoken attitude towards the Pope and the Church of Rome, Savonarola truly believed that he was acting in the best interests of the people, so he was quick to try to back-pedal his way out of the excommunication, writing a rather grovelling letter to Alexander in which he asked why the Pope was so angry with him. But Savonarola, ever the snake when it came to his views about His Holiness, also condemned the excommunication in an another open, harshly worded letter in which he clearly said that he was: 'Sent by Jesus Christ to the city of Florence to announce the advent of the great scourging of Italy and above all of Rome, which is then to spread to almost all the world in our days and soon.'[5]

He was convinced that he had done nothing wrong; that he had simply preached the word of God. One of the biggest reasons behind his excommunication was that Savonarola and his followers had refused to join the new Tuscan Congregation – which had been put together to silence him – but he claimed Rome had forgotten that he had offered a full explanation for his reasons behind the refusal. More importantly, Rome did not even bother to reply to his explanation.

Eventually the Pope offered him a way out under two conditions: that he travel to Rome and prostrate himself before the Pope and seek forgiveness, and that he join with the Tuscan Congregation. Of course Savonarola refused. Agreeing to these demands would turn everything he had worked for on its head. Instead he made good use of the excommunication and his ban on preaching by sitting in his cell within the walls of San Marco and writing – expanding on his previous theological and philosophical works such as *The Triumph of the Cross*.

When Bernardo del Nero took over as the gonfalonier, it worried Savonarola. The man was fervently opposed to the friar and his supporters. Still, at this point, Savonarola had just enough followers in the Signoria to keep the wolves at bay. Yet the election of this man who so despised the prior of San Marco gave hope to those who supported the restitution of the Medici.

Savonarola and the government were highly aware of the threat Piero posed to the city. Despite his dislike of the friar, Bernardo del Nero had to swallow his pride for the good of protecting Florence. Besides, what was coming would set of a course of events that would please not only del Nero but all of those who hated Savonarola. While Piero had been working on raising an army, the government had been working on protecting the city and had arrested a number of people they suspected of being involved in his plot. Despite its failure to take back the city,

Lamberto dell'Antella, who was arrested while carrying secret messages out of Florence on Piero's behest, confessed all and agreed to give the government names of those who had been involved. To widespread shock, the names he coughed up were those of some of the most powerful men in Florence. Bernardo Cambo and Giannozzo Pucci under torture, gave more names of those who had some knowledge of Medici's plans to take the city. Of the names proffered, the most high profile was Bernardo del Nero, and he was joined by two other prominent men – Lorenzo Tornabuoni and Niccolò Ridolfi. These three were arrested immediately and put to torture. Nero, 72, admitted without hesitation that he had been aware of Piero's plans. The five men were sentenced to death, but the Signoria were split about whether or not they should be allowed to appeal. Arguments ensued and eventually it was decided that they would not be granted their appeal and the executions went forward with startling speed. Within moments of the final decision being reached, priests were called to hear the last confessions of the condemned men, and their wives and children were allowed a brief visit to say their goodbyes. The five men were then beheaded in the courtyard of the Bargello prison with del Nero being the last to die. It took five blows of the axe to remove his head, the last removing the old man's chin.[6]

After the execution, rumours abounded that Savonarola had some hand in getting rid of these men; but this was at odds with his morals. Nevertheless, his enemies used the allegations to further blacken his name. It did not matter that previously Savonarola had asked for mercy in similar cases of execution. Nor did it matter that he said he would not get involved in politics. For the Mediceans this was just another thing to hold against him.

Savonarola was still under the order of excommunication and so was not preaching. His supporters, however, lobbied for the bull to be withdrawn – in October 1497 they convinced him to write a submissive letter to Alexander, begging for forgiveness and professing his innocence. He agreed and his missive could not have been more deferential:

I am more distressed at having your Holiness' favour withdrawn from me than by any other misfortune and fly eagerly to your feet, begging you to hear my cry at last and no longer let me be torn from your bosom. To whom else can I go as one of his flock except to the shepherds whose voice I love to hear, whose blessings I implore? I would go at once to cast myself at your feet if only I could be safe on the journey from my enemies, malice and plots. As soon as I can do so without danger I shall set out at once and wish with all my heart that I could do it now in order to prove myself innocent of these calumnies once and for all.[7]

Of course, Savonarola made absolutely no effort to go to Rome and throw himself at the pontiff's feet. Despite his stubborn refusal to acquiesce to the Pope's requests, he still believed the two could be reconciled. But although his friends in Rome had put in good words for him, nothing had come of it. When the subject of Savonarola came up, Alexander snapped that the friar had insulted the honour of the Holy See, and thus the honour of the Borgia Pope. They were at a point now where there seemed to be no turning back.

When, by the end of 1497, the Pope still had not lifted the excommunication, Savonarola lost his patience and, on Christmas Day, he decided it was time to come out from his self-imposed exile. (At least in his mind it was self-imposed – to anyone else, it was him abiding by the excommunication order to please the Pope.) He celebrated by giving communion at San Marco. His first sermon was 11 February 1498 – yet as Savonarola was still under excommunication, people were not allowed to go and see him preach, a crucial fact that the canons of the Duomo repeated to members of the Signoria. The canon who delivered this message was forced to resign and be replaced by someone who supported the friar.

The sermon dealt, as could only be expected, with Savonarola's recent falling out with Rome and even mentioned that the recent murder of Pope Alexander's favoured son, Juan Borgia, Duke of Gandia, who was found in the River Tiber with his throat slit, was punishment for the Pope's vices and sins. His main question was, 'tell me this, what was the object of those who used lying to get me excommunicated?'[8] Already walking a thin line, his sermons only got more heated. On Ash Wednesday, he preached before a large crowd:

> Oh Rome, Rome! You're going to suffer so much; you'll be sorry you ever fought us. You call yourselves blessed while we are the excommunicated although you fight as the damned do, like infidels. Rome should realise that the friar in Florence and his followers want to fight you evil men in the same way we would fight the Turks, that we want to die and suffer martyrdom. Yes, I really want to be martyred by you. Oh Lord, grant me this grace! You think you can frighten me, Rome, but I don't know the meaning of fear.[9]

One has to wonder if he would later regret these comments about martyrdom.

This was becoming more than a war of words. More letters and briefs came from Rome which said the Pope was aware that Savonarola had started preaching again and, more importantly, that he knew the vitriol he was spouting. The letters came with an order that the friar be sent to Rome, and if he repented his crimes, then the Pope would treat him kindly. The canons of Santa Maria del Fiore were also ordered to stop Savonarola from entering the cathedral. This back and forth with Alexander, as well as the election of another anti-Savonarolan gonfalonier, kept knocking the friar back. With every passing day his position grew weaker, but still the Signoria dithered about what they should say to the Pope in reply to his briefs. In the end they told him that at the moment they could not risk making a move against the friar – he was still far too popular and if they reacted negatively, his supporters could very easily rise against them.

He wrote letters to the crowned heads of Europe:

> The moment of vengeance has come and the Lord commands me to reveal new secrets, making clear to the world the danger that threatens the Barque of Peter because of your neglect. The Church is full of abominations, from the crown of her head to the soles of her feet, yet not only do you fail to apply any sort of cure but you even pay

homage to the source of the evils that pollute her. In consequence, the Lord is deeply angered and for a long time has left the Church without a shepherd.

Now I hereby testify, *in verbo Domini*, that this Alexander is no Pope, nor can he be considered one because – leaving aside the sin of simony by which he bought the Papal Chair and sells the Church benefices to the highest bidder every day, and ignoring his all other too obvious vices – I declare that he is not a Christian and does not believe in the existence of God, which goes beyond the bounds of infidelity. [10]

While many of the letters did not reach their intended recipients, one of the two intended for the king of France was stolen on the way and sold to Ludovico Sforza of Milan. Sforza, immediately realising how important the information was, passed the letter to the Pope. Finally, Alexander had the irrefutable proof that he had so desperately wanted. Girolamo Savonarola was a traitor to him and the Church of Rome. It was time for the papacy to make a move – and it would come about in the most remarkable of circumstances.

The friar's enemies were growing bolder, and one of the most outspoken was Francesco di Puglia who lived in the monastery of Santa Croce. Puglia had previously spoken out about Savonarola and challenged him, or any of his supporters, to take part in an ordeal by fire. This involved the two opposing competitors walking along a passageway through a blazing bonfire. Whoever came out of the other side untouched by the flames was the one God smiled upon and, thus, the winner. On the same day that Puglia issued that challenge, one of Savonarola's followers, Fra Domenica da Pescia, was in the congregation and he was enthusiastic about taking up the challenge. But before he could accept, Puglia was ordered back to Florence after word reached his superiors of his plan, and he returned to Santa Croce with his tail between his legs. The whole idea of an ordeal by fire was, for the moment, forgotten. That was, until Savonarola delivered a sermon in which he unwittingly reminded Puglia of the plan, saying: 'I entreat each one of you to pray earnestly to God that if my doctrine does not come from Him, He will send down a fire upon me, which shall consume my soul in Hell.'[11]

Francesco di Puglia immediately began shouting from his pulpit that he was once again challenging the Dominican to trial by fire. Evidently Savonarola found the idea laughable and simply ignored him. But while Savonarola refused to engage, his fellow Dominican, Domenico da Pescia, again cried out that he was ready to step into the inferno to prove that Savonarola was indeed chosen by God. Puglia had claimed that he was willing to die to prove that Savonarola was a fraud and to rid the city of his heretical ways, but when he heard that Pescia would be taking his place, he decided he was not going to take part after all, insisting that he only had an argument with Savonarola, not with Pescia. The whole thing should have come to a stop there – however the Signoria had become involved and had come to the conclusion that an ordeal by fire was the perfect way to get rid of the friar.

Pescia's over-enthusiasm was, unfortunately for Savonarola, playing into the Signoria's hands. Savonarola warned him not to get involved but Pescia went ahead and published a statement on his belief in Savonarola, which was called *Conclusiones*. He wrote:

> The Church of God needs to be reformed, it must be scourged and renovated. Likewise, Florence too must be scourged before it can be renovated and return to prosperity. The infidels must be converted to Christianity. All these things will come to pass in our time. The excommunication issued against the reverend father our brother Hieronymo is invalid. Those who choose to ignore this excommunication are not sinners.[12]

This was precisely what Savonarola's enemies, the Arabbiati and Compagnacci needed. Until this point, they had no solid proof of Savonarola's defiance against the excommunication and orders that had come down from Rome – but here it was in writing. Shortly after its publication, the Signoria summoned Pescia to the Palazzo della Signoria to prove that the writing and signature were his and, once confirmed, Puglia was finally persuaded to admit that Pescia had accepted his challenge. He signed to say that he acknowledged it and the stage was set for a showdown. It became even more interesting when another Dominican – Fra Mariano Ughi – stepped forward and said that he would happily accompany his colleague through the flames.

Savonarola and his acolytes were about to enter their final chapters.

# Chapter 11

# The Ordeal by Fire and the Siege of San Marco

The date chosen for the ordeal was 6 April but it was then moved to the following day, the Saturday before Palm Sunday. Work began on putting together the walkway and the bonfire, which the chosen two would walk through. Along the side of the walkway, which stretched for over 300 metres across the Piazza della Signoria, logs were stacked. They were covered in brushwood, branches and twigs that were coated in oil and pitch. Stuffed between the logs and the walkway was earth, bricks and rubble to keep the flames from the beams that held it up. The passage itself was narrow, barely big enough for the two to pass each other. One had to come out the winner and one had to be consigned to the flames.

The day dawned and both the Franciscans and Dominicans spent the early hours in prayer. Later on that morning, the macebearers of the Signoria went to each of the parties to inform them that all was ready, and it was time for them to face their ordeal. The Franciscans flocked to the piazza where they were placed in the southernmost area of the square. This had been split into two separate areas – a pen for the Franciscans, and one for the Dominicans. However, Puglia and the monk he had chosen to walk through the flames on his behalf were not among the men crammed into the square – they were inside the palazzo, holding more talks with the government.

The piazza soon became full of people who wanted to see if Savonarola could perform some sort of miracle. The previous day, it had been ordered that all foreigners, with the exception of hired soldiers, leave the city. The gates to the city had been locked and the gateway to the piazza barricaded. Soldiers were placed all around the square to keep order amongst the citizens desperate to see the show. Women and children were not allowed in, but they could be seen watching from windows and rooftops of the buildings that surrounded the piazza.

While the Franciscans had already arrived in the square and waited patiently for the ordeal to begin, the Dominicans made a spectacle out of their arrival. They emerged in a procession – about 250 friars led the way, walking in twos, and were followed by the man who would enter the flames on Savonarola's behalf, Fra Domenico da Pescia, who carried a large crucifix and was flanked by two friars. He also wore a red velvet cape – red was a symbol of rage, martyrdom, fire and Hell. Did Pescia believe he would die as a martyr in this ordeal, or could he have been showing his contempt for his rival by wearing the colour that represented his challenger's eventual outcome – burning to death in the flames? Savonarola walked behind Pescia and in his hands he carried a box that held the Host, the consecrated body of Christ. Behind Savonarola were men and children as well as women holding lit candles, but they had to stay back – only the friars were allowed in the square. The diarist Landucci recorded the moment the Dominicans entered the arena:

And then came the Dominicans, with the greatest show of devotion. There was a great number of Frati, about 250, walking in pairs, followed by Fra Domenico bearing a crucifix, and then Fra Girolamo holding aloft the Host; whilst behind them was a great multitude with torches and candles, devoutly singing hymns. After they had taken their place in the Loggia and prepared an altar, they sang a mass and the people awaited the great spectacle.[1]

The crowd bustled with excitement, hoping the show would get started quickly, but they were disappointed. The Franciscans took umbrage at the fact that Pescia was wearing the red velvet cloak and said they believed it was bewitched. He was made to remove it. The Dominicans then decided the robes he had on underneath the cape could be bewitched as well, so he was made to change robes with another friar. They then argued about him taking his crucifix into the flames, saying that it could also be bewitched.

Savonarola willingly gave this point to the Franciscans and suggested that Domenico carry a piece of the Host into the flames instead. But the Franciscans took umbrage at that as well, saying that it was heresy to carry such a holy thing into the fire. Representatives were pulled into the palazzo and took part in a theological debate on the matter, keeping the crowd waiting even longer. One can only imagine how irritable the people were becoming. They had flocked to the square to watch what they hoped would be a sensational drama; a battle of life and death. Instead they were being forced to wait as others bickered, and their patience was wearing thin. Even Savonarola was becoming impatient as he was aware the mood of the people was shifting. He sent a message into the palazzo asking the debaters to hurry it up. They responded saying that if he was so desperate for the ordeal to go ahead, he could walk through the flames himself. Of course he declined the invitation. As the wait continued, the mood in the piazza grew ever more tense and a small riot broke out in one corner which had to be put down by the soldiers surrounding the square. Could anyone blame them? Many had been waiting since dawn and there had been no explanation for the delay. To make matters worse, the weather suddenly changed. The heavens opened and a downpour soaked the pyre.

Then the doors of the palazzo opened, and it was announced that the ordeal would not be taking place. The crowd, already restless, lost their temper and began to shout that the friar had made fools of them. It did not take long for the gathering to turn into an angry mob, being goaded by Savonarola's enemies who were assembled there too. The friar and his fellow Dominicans had to fight their way back to San Marco, where they believed they would be safe.

It soon became clear that they were the furthest thing from safe, and having failed to deliver the promised show, Savonarola knew that he had lost the confidence of the people. Perhaps he had even earned their hatred after the shambles of the day. As the Dominicans hid behind their walls and sang a *Te Deum*, giving thanks for their safe return to the monastery, it was becoming obvious the mob was gearing up to attack their home. They were allowed a short amount of respite, however, as the trouble did not begin until the next day with a riot at Santa Maria del Fiore when anti-Savonarolans tried to stop Dominican friars from giving a sermon within the cathedral. Landucci recorded the chaos:

> [Savonarola's enemies] began to strike the backs of the seats where the women were sitting, using rough language, and saying: '*Andate con Dio, piagnonacci*' ['Go away, go away, you whining old psalms-mongers'], so that many stood up, and there was a great tumult in the church, anyone who could find the door being lucky.[2]

As insults were hurled, people began to panic and run for the doors. Stones were thrown, which hailed back to the old stone-throwing fights on the Ponte Vecchio during Carnevale that had been banned by Savonarola. The violence spilled out into the streets where not only Savonarola was threatened directly, anyone who even looked as though they supported him was attacked. Landucci went on to describe the events:

> The adversaries of the Frate, especially the Compagnia de Compagnacci, rushing towards the convent cried 'A' Frati, a' Frati, a San Marco!' And all the people and the children joined them and ran along with stones, making it impossible for many men and women who were in San Marco to come out ... if I had not managed to get out through the cloister, and go away towards the Porta di San Gallo, I might have been killed. Everyone was arming himself, in fact; and a proclamation from the *Palagio* offered 1000 ducats to anyone who should capture Fra Girolamo and deliver him up to the authorities. All Florence was in a commotion, and none of the frate's adherents dared to speak, or else they would have been killed.[3]

The mob was coming, and the Dominicans began to make ready to protect their home, the monastery. Within the walls along with the friars, were a number of Savonarola's most staunch supporters including the former gonfalonier, Francesco Valori. He had tried to take the sensible route, advising the friars not to resort to violence as it was totally against the vows they had made. But the group of Dominicans had their minds made up – if their home was to be attacked, then they would defend it with their lives. Two of them, Fra Silvestro and Fra Francesco de' Medici, had even stashed weapons away in a disused cell in case something like this were ever to happen. It was certainly forward thinking on their part. They had managed to collect 'twelve breastplates and a similar number of helmets; eighteen halberds, five or six crossbows, various shields, four or five arquebuses, a barrel of gunpowder and a crate of leaden bullets, as well as a couple of small primitive mortars.'[4]

The weapons were just the start. Two of Savonarola's leading supporters, Francesco Davanzati and Baldo Inghirami, began to plan a staunch defence of the monastery. This involved guards and watchmen being placed along the walls, handing out arms and organising friars who were willing to take up the weapons. The huge, heavy doors leading into San Marco were locked and its inhabitants were ready to fight should it come to that. Savonarola would have been horrified had he known all of this preparation going on right under his nose, given his views on violence. It is not known whether he refused to believe this was happening inside his home while the mob began to congregate outside the walls, or whether he was actually ignorant of the plans afoot.

The crowd was getting rowdy. Missiles, including rocks and stinking refuse, were thrown over the walls of the complex. These actions resulted in the friars, very probably ordered by their leader, ringing the monastery bell that was usually used to summon people to service in the church. This time it was used as a warning bell and acted as a call for help. But help did not come. The Signoria had taken the side of the mob, and had sent their macebearer to San Marco to order that the monks stop fighting. They also ordered that Savonarola go into exile and be out of Florentine territory within twelve hours. But he and his supporters did not take the threat seriously. They thought it had not really come from the Signoria and was a ruse to make them open up the gates, so the crowd could rush in and take their revenge on the friar whom they suddenly seemed to despise.

When the Signoria realised they were being ignored, they argued about what action should be taken against the errant Dominicans. As they discussed the matter, Savonarola tried to convince those in San Marco that violence should be avoided. He announced that he would take a crucifix and walk out of the monastery, surrendering himself to those who were calling for his arrest. It was only when his friars begged him not to go, crying that he would be torn apart, that he changed his mind.

As darkness descended on Florence, the scenes of brutality outside the monastery got worse. Landucci described it in his diary, with a particularly awful description of what happened to Francesco Valori as he escaped from the besieged monastery:

> Francesco Valori came out of San Marco secretly into the garden at the back and along by the walls, where he was seized by two wretched men and taken to his house. Later in the evening he was fetched by the macebearers of the Signoria, who promised that his life should be spared, and led him away to the *Palagio*. On the way, however, when they were near San Procolo … a man came up behind him and struck him on the head with a billhook two or three times, so that he died on the spot. And when they pillaged his house, they had wounded his wife so that she died, and they also wounded the children and their nurses, robbing everything.[5]

The friars had been waiting expectantly for Valori to return, oblivious to the fact that he had been murdered. As they waited, the mob around San Marco grew larger and more violent. Landucci described the moment they finally managed to breach San Marco: 'At about 6 in the night [2 am] they set fire to the doors of the church and the cloister of San Marco and penetrating into the church began to fight.'[6]

The monks forgot their vows of peace and fought back using the weapons they had stored away. One friar even brandished an arquebus and, stationing himself in the pulpit of the church, managed to shoot and kill several of the enemy. But as the violence raged around him, Savonarola refused to join in and tried to curb the chaos with the only weapon he possessed. He stationed himself in the library of San Marco, on the top floor of the monastery, and announced to those who had gathered with him that he was planning to surrender. Knowing that he was serious, many of his followers begged to go with him when he handed himself over, but in the end he decided that only one would be allowed to go with him – Fra Domenico da Pescia, whose faith in him had been staggeringly unwavering. Then, in the monastery library, he addressed his followers and gave them what can only be described as a goodbye:

> All I have said came to me from God, and He is my witness in heaven that I am not lying. I hadn't foreseen that the city would turn against me so soon, but may the Lord's will be done. My final command to you is this – let faith, prayer and patience be your weapons. I am leaving you with grief and anguish, to surrender myself into the hands of my enemies. I don't know if they will kill me, but you can be certain that once I'm dead I shall be able to help you better in heaven than I have been on earth. Take comfort, embrace the cross and through it you'll find salvation.[7]

By the time he had delivered his speech, the Signoria had finally decided to send an armed contingent to the monastery. This group of soldiers had managed to get the rabble in order and the leader, Giovanni della Vecchia, pushed his way through to the breached cloisters. He was greeted by the friars who agreed to hand over Savonarola: 'Finally, while the Frate was in the chancel singing the office, two Frati came out and said: "We will agree to give up the Frate to you, if you will take him to the *Palagio* in safety" and this was promised.'[8]

Vecchia assured the friars that their leader would be kept safe and then Savonarola, along with Domenico da Pescia, appeared in the cloister where they were arrested by Vecchia and the macebearers of the Signoria. They were placed in irons and led away to the palazzo, walking through the angry crowd who surged at them, screaming insults in their faces. As he was ushered into the palazzo, one man managed to land a blow to Savonarola's backside shouting, 'There's the seat of his prophecies!'[9]

Fra Silvestro Maruffi, an ardent supporter of Savonarola, had also been ordered to be arrested. In the confusion, he had managed to hide himself away but his location had been given to the Signoria by Malatesta

Sacramoro, a Dominican friar who had betrayed his brothers and gone over to the other side in an effort to align himself with the winners. The wayward Maruffi was also taken into custody joining his two colleagues in the cells within the Palazzo della Signoria.

Savonarola and Pescia were ushered, beaten and bruised by the crowd baying for their blood, into the apparent safety of the Palazzo della Signoria. They were separated and locked up, with Savonarola imprisoned in a small cell at the top of the palazzo's tower – this cell, known as the *alberghettino* or 'little inn' was where important prisoners were kept. Previously, Cosimo de' Medici had been imprisoned in the cell with its tiny window that looked out over the city. Savonarola must have had some idea of the trouble that he was in as he languished here, in that his goodbye speech declared he was not sure if he would live or die. Yet, as a religious man, he must have had some sort of faith that God would save him and the people of Florence would come back into the fold and plead for his release. He would be sadly disappointed.

# Chapter 12

# 'I may easily die if you torture me more'

It was obvious that there was no way Savonarola was going to be treated fairly or kindly. The first clue was the way he was hauled in irons up to the *alberghettino*. The second was when he was taken from there to the infamous Bargello, the prison just a stone's throw away from the Palazzo della Signoria. It was within these walls that horrific torture took place, as well as executions. Construction began in 1255, although the building itself was not called the Bargello until the sixteenth century when it was the police station (*bargello* means police station[1]), and the home of the chief of police. An imposing building, it is clear just from looking at it that it was built to withstand attack *and* keep people inside.

Savonarola would probably have expected to be tortured while being questioned here – after all, it was the usual way of extracting a confession from a prisoner and was, in fact, the due process of law. However, this 'due process' would end up being little more than a kangaroo court in which the friar's confession would simply be what his interrogators wanted to hear.

The only problem was that the Signoria rushed in. They actually had no legal standing to begin the process of torture so quickly. The Signoria should have waited for permission to arrive from Rome, which did not happen until 12 April. However, Savonarola was initially questioned on being taken to the Bargello, when physical force was used in order to extract the desired information – that his preaching was lies. Landucci described events in his diaries:

At 9 in the evening [5 pm] the Frate was carried to the Bargello by two men on their crossed hands, because his feet and hands were in irons ... and put Fra Girolamo to the rack three times ... and Fra Girolamo said: 'Take me down, and I will write you my whole life.'[2]

Write everything down he did, but his interrogators were far from satisfied. So they questioned him again. He held up under duress, defending his words and his preaching – he would, in essence, confess to nothing. He was subjected to a method of torture that was well known in Florence, and often used on prisoners – the *strappado*:

> He was hoisted some distance from the floor, then allowed to fall rapidly, and the rope being suddenly checked with a jerk, his arms were forced back until they described a half-circle, his muscles lacerated, and all his limbs quivering with pain. The torture of the rope and pulley, when slightly applied was by no means one of the most cruel but could sometimes be used in a way to overcome the strongest frame and the firmest endurance. When continued for any length of time it invariably produced delirium, sometimes ending in death; consequently the sufferer could be made to confess anything. It was only a matter of time.[3]

This kind of persecution was designed to extract any 'confession' out of its victim. But the friar did not break and continued to say that his preaching was true. They made him write his 'confession' which, when they read it, was not to their liking so they destroyed every page. The torture and examination would have to start again, so he was taken back to his cell at the top of the palazzo's bell tower and there he knelt and prayed, saying that his torturers had no idea what they were doing.

The man appointed as Savonarola's torturer, and the man given the job of obtaining his confession, was a government notary named Francesco de Ser Barone – known by the nickname Ser Ceccone. An ardent supporter of Piero de' Medici, he was believed to be perfect for the job, given the fact he had acted as a spy from within the walls of San Marco and attended every single one of Savonarola's sermons, pretending to be a 'supporter'. The Signoria were happy to overlook the fact that he was a mere notary, and thus not legally allowed to perform torture on a prisoner.

The next part of the interrogation took part over the best part of a week, coming to an end on 17 April. The work did not even stop over the Easter weekend, proving just how desperate the Signoria were to get Savonarola to talk.

It did not take long for news of Savonarola's arrest to reach Rome. Just forty-eight hours after he was taken into custody, Alexander VI was informed of what had happened and sent a letter to the Signoria, praising their actions:

> It gave us the greatest pleasure when your ambassador informed us of the timely measures you have taken in order to crush the mad vindictiveness of that son of iniquity Fra Hieronymo Savonarola .... At last he is safely imprisoned, which causes us to give praise to our beloved Saviour.[4]

Alexander went on to grant explicit permission for the friar to be tortured – which was meaningless, as they had already started torturing him – and stated that once they had finished, he was to be taken to Rome where he would face an ecclesiastical tribunal. This trial would, of course, involve more than just the *strappado*. Not only did that please the Signoria greatly, but the Pope's dispatch also freed Florence from the previous excommunication, which would have also been warmly received. However, the Signoria were reluctant to send Savonarola to Rome in case he told his interrogators the secrets he had learned of the Florentine government. So he was kept in Florence, where his trial was conducted in absolute secrecy, something which greatly displeased Alexander.

The trial continued with Savonarola being subjected to multiple drops of the *strappado*. Ser Ceccone made a record of what he uncovered during the torture. While the original transcript does not exist, later copies show that Ceccone deliberately skewed what Savonarola had told him during the sessions. Of course this is to be expected – twisting the facts to make out the prisoner was guiltier than he actually was came as no surprise. Skewed facts, along with some admissions, would only make the friar seem more guilty. Some of the text reads:

In the two years I preached there [San Gimignano] I proposed these conclusions, that the Church was to be scourged. Since I did not have this by revelation but from reasons derived from scripture ... . So, as my desire and eagerness to preach such things grew, I became more ardent to reaffirm them in some way. Seeing it all go well, and my reputation and favour among the Florentines grow, I went further and began to say that I had it from revelation, although in fact it was all the invention of my zeal ... . I did not talk with God, nor God with me, in the special way in which he speaks to his holy apostles.[5]

During this initial stage of the interrogation, Ceccone asked Savonarola to confess that he was not a prophet, and that his claims to have spoken directly with God were false. According to Ceccone, Savonarola refused. If he had not, it would have been a huge admission. However, it is entirely possible that under torture he would have admitted this – he would have admitted to anything under such circumstances. As such, can the transcripts of the friar's trial be a trustworthy source? They certainly show a bias that allowed both the Florentine government and the Pope to get their wish, whether what had been written down was based on truth or not.

Ceccone then drew up a deposition which the friar signed. It was read out publicly and Landucci recorded the event in his diaries:

I was present when this protocol was read, and I marvelled feeling utterly dumbfounded with surprise. My heart was grieved to see such an edifice fall to the ground on account of having been founded on a lie. Florence had been expecting a new Jerusalem, from which would issue just laws and splendour and an example of righteous life, and to see the renovation of the church, the conversion of non-unbelievers and the consolation of the righteous; and I felt that everything was exactly contrary, and had to resign myself to the thought: *In voluntate tua Domine omnia sunt posita.*[6]

The deposition, however, was generally not believed and made Savonarola seem almost entirely innocent. The Signoria tried desperately to stop it from circulating and sent a letter to Alexander claiming that the friar had not confessed as he was astonishingly tolerant to pain.

Ercole, Duke of Ferrara, wrote to the Signoria to ask mercy for the friar. He was a son of Ferrara after all. But the letter was ignored. The Florentines were determined to extract a confession, so the torture continued, not only of Savonarola but two other friars had also been subjected to horrendous abuse. Fra Domenico da Pescia, who had been so staunchly supportive of Savonarola, had been arrested alongside the friar after the siege of San Marco as well as Fra Silvestro Maruffi, who had been arrested after trying to escape the monastery.

Pescia was subjected to more than just the *strappado*. While he did face the drops, he proved to be so stubborn that they decided to use the iron boot (*stanghetta*) on him as well. This involved iron ankle bracelets being tightened to cause extreme pain and, if continued for too long, the rapid onset of gangrene.[7] Yet still he remained silent, refusing to tell his interrogators what they wanted to hear; instead he said that if they continued to torture him, they would simply kill him: 'I may easily die if you torture me more, because I am so shattered that my arms are useless, especially the left one which …is dislocated for a second time.'[8]

The torturers persisted, and still he remained resolute, refusing to speak out against the leader of the Dominicans. He was steadfast in his support of Savonarola, despite his ordeal. The words of his first deposition are particularly heart wrenching and show a man who believed wholeheartedly in Savonarola:

Our Lord Jesus Christ knows that I, Fra' Domenico, bound here for His sake, speak no falseness on any of these matters … . I came with the firm resolve to go through [the ordeal by fire] nor did I think that any objection would be made to my bearing the Host … . If therefore, this gave rise to scandal, God, by whose will I accepted the Ordeal, will grant me His reward.[9]

Fra Silvestro Maruffi did not fare as well under torture, proving himself to be the sort of man who broke easily under pressure. He was willing to save his own life, at the expense of Savonarola's. He did as he was asked and denounced the friar, as well as a number of other men who had visited him in San Marco. Sadly for him, however, much of the information he provided was insufficient to help build any sort of charge against Savonarola. He said:

> As regards my own opinion of Fra' Girolamo's deeds, I may say that on twenty or twenty five different occasions when he was about to preach, he would come, before the sermon, to my cell, and say to me: 'I know not what to preach, pray thou to God for me, since I fear that He may have forsaken me on account of my sins.' And he would say that he wished to unburden his soul, and accordingly make confession, and nevertheless would afterwards preach beautiful sermons. And the last time he did this was on the Saturday before the last Sunday he preached in St. Mark's this Lent. Finally, I say that he deceived us.[10]

He was not the only one of Savonarola's followers to turn against their leader. Many said they had been deceived and deluded by the frate and wrote letters to the Pope to plead for his forgiveness, begging him to lift the burden of excommunication from their shoulders.

The debate continued as to whether or not Savonarola and his two accomplices should be sent to Rome to face judgement. However the majority of men within the Signoria believed that Savonarola should be executed in Florence, the city which he had duped so badly. The general view was that if it were to happen in Rome, it would become a spectacle, whereas if it took place in Florence, it could happen relatively quietly and then, once it was done, it could be forgotten about. While this went against the Pope's wishes, they made him an offer to ensure he was involved in the process. They said that while Savonarola being executed in Florence would help deter his followers, Alexander was more than welcome to send his own men to interrogate the Dominican.

This invitation satisfied Alexander, who sent word that he no longer required the friar to be taken to Rome and decided that the Signoria could tax ecclesiastical property within the city for three years, which was unprecedented. He then chose two commissioners to go to Florence and interrogate Savonarola, along with orders that, after they found him guilty, they were to strip him and his two colleagues of their place in the Church so that they could be executed by the secular arm of the law. Both sides would then be able to get what they wanted – Savonarola dead. The first man chosen to interrogate Savonarola on behalf of the Church was Master General of the Dominican Order, Fra Gioacchino Torriano. He was not to play an active role in the proceedings however, having until recently been a close friend of the accused friar. The other commissioner was a crony of Alexander's, a Catalan named Francisco de Remolins – known more familiarly as Remolino – and a formidable canon lawyer. Alexander trusted Remolino implicitly and knew that he would be able to get a result.

The morning after the two commissioners arrived in Florence, Remolino brought together the torturers for a fresh session with the accused. This time a number of Florentine officials were invited to watch. That way, they could keep an eye on what was going on and make sure that the officials from Rome got what they wanted.

But Savonarola proved tricky. In the time since his previous interrogation, he had evidently regained some of his strength and, rather than succumb to almost certain death, he decided to play games with his inquisitors. Questioned about his previous confession, the friar answered with part truth to hide his real answer, but never fully lied. Remolino's patience ran out very quickly at this, and he threatened Savonarola with more torture. It had the desired effect, and effectively broke him. This part of the transcript from the trial details the friar's reaction:

'Now hearken to my words, O God! Thou hast rejected me.' Here he fell to his knees saying: 'I confess that I have denied Christ. I have spoken lies. O Signoria of Florence, I have denied Him from dread of torture. If I have to suffer, I will suffer for the truth. That which I have said came to me from God. O God Thou dost impose penance on me for having denied Thee. I deserve it. I have denied Thee. I have denied Thee for fear of torments! … Jesus aid me; this time Thou hast found out my sins.'[11]

Girolamo Savonarola, a man who had once seemed untouchable, was broken. One can only imagine the fear of further torture that had caused him to break down in such a way. That was what made the *strappado* ingenious – it caused immense pain, yet death was rare, hence it often worked well in getting confessions out of prisoners. It probably did not help that Remolino was a master at torturing admissions out of his victims, having learned the craft in Rome, probably picking up tips from his friend, Cesare Borgia. To Remolino, this was a game. A game that he was winning each time he asked a question and got an answer from the terrified friar. The questions came thick and fast, with Savonarola answering just how Remolino wanted. 'Why do you call upon Jesus?', Remolino asked only to be answered with, 'So I seem like a good man.' When the interrogator continued, Savonarola broke down again, begging, 'Do not torture me any further. I will tell the truth.' Still Remolino played his game, like a cat with a mouse. 'Why did you deny what you had already confessed?' he asked. Savonarola's answer was simple and utterly heartbreaking – 'Because I am a fool.'[12]

When Savonarola was eventually lowered from the *strappado* after this round of questioning, he said that if he was allowed to be in a room with those who treated him well, he would be able to talk reasonably without losing grip of himself, as he did when threatened with torture. Of course, Remolino was far too clever for this and continued asking a series of questions which seemed to be inconsequential but had been loaded in a way to make the friar trip up and condemn himself. 'Have you ever preached that Jesus Christ was just a man?' he asked. Had Savonarola answered this wrongly, he could have easily been charged with heresy, yet he bit back with: 'Only a fool would ever think such a thing.' Other dangerous questions followed, all aimed at getting Savonarola to slip up, yet he just about managed to hold himself upright. One was, 'Do you believe in magic charms?', and the reply given was, 'I have always derided such nonsense.'[13]

While Remolino was questioning Savonarola on the issue of the Church council he had called for and the cardinals who were believed to be in cahoots with him, the Signoria came together to discuss the sentence that would be imposed on the friar. While there were some who believed that he should not be charged and executed, the majority within the room supported the idea of putting him to death. They knew that, as members of government changed every two months, if they failed to act immediately, a future government would end up setting him free. That was something they could not have happen – they were afraid of Savonarola and his followers. More so, they were afraid of what would happen if evidence of his trials ever got out into the public eye with proof that Ceccone had tampered with the evidence. This was elaborated on sometime later in an exchange between the artist Sandro Botticelli and Doffo Spini, a member of the Florentine government who had been part of Savonarola's interrogations. When Botticelli asked Spini about what had happened, the reply was stark: 'We found no sin in him, moral or venial … . [If we had not condemned Savonarola] the mob would have put us all in a sack, torn to pieces. The business stirred up too much hatred – we condemned them to save our own skins.'[14]

One last short interrogation of Savonarola by Remolino took place on 22 May. Following this brief meeting, a message was dispatched to the prisoner ordering him to appear before the commission the following day, where his trial would finally be concluded, and his sentence served. Exhausted and terrified, Savonarola sent back a message saying, 'I am in prison, if I am able, I will come.' Remolino then met with the Florentine government to agree the fate of not only Savonarola, but of Pescia and Maruffi who had been interrogated alongside their master, although neither of them had been questioned by the papal commissioners. Remolino argued that Domenico, who was seen to be nothing but saintly, should be spared. But the Signoria would not hear of it and Remolino seemed to shrug his shoulders and agree that one less friar would not hurt. Pescia would join his master and Maruffi on the scaffold.

Remolino then locked himself away to compile a report for Alexander. Probably written entirely by Remolino, it was signed by him and Torriano and was evidently compiled to blacken the name of Savonarola even further. The report was full of lies and libel, as this extract shows:

First, Fra' Hieronymo admits that for fourteen years he never confessed his sins properly yet went on saying Mass. Further, he declares that he arranged for Fra' Silvestro and many other friars to hear confessions and report to him what they found out and that afterwards, publicly in the pulpit and privately in conversation, he denounced the sins made known to him in this way, pretending that he knew of them by divine revelation. In addition, he has committed such grave and detestable crimes that for the moment it would be wrong to mention them. He confesses to spreading sedition among the citizens, to causing food shortages which have resulted in the death of the poor, and to murdering many people of rank.[15]

Remolino was showing just why Alexander could trust him – he had absolutely no issue in twisting the truth to get the desired outcome. It mattered little that Savonarola was not the evil heretic that people wanted him to be. What mattered was getting a result and getting rid of the thorn in Pope Alexander's side. The report goes on:

He also confesses that, through letters and messages, he tried to urge Christian princes into schism against your Holiness. To such depths of wickedness did this most evil and many sided monster sink that his entire appearance of goodness was merely pretended, a disguise for his ambition and thirst to gain glory in this world. He has been accustomed to turning the crucifix and saying to our Lord, 'If I lie, then you lie.' So enormous are his crimes that the hand shrinks from writing them down, the mind from contemplating them.[16]

And so the lies continued.

The three friars were finally condemned as heretics and schismatics on 22 May 1498. The sentence passed was the worst possible – they were to be degraded, which is to say that they would be stripped of their place within the Church hierarchy, before being hanged and burned, while still alive, on a specially made scaffold. The execution was to happen in the Piazza della Signoria before a throng of citizens. Landucci described the public preparation for the spectacle:

> In the evening a scaffold was made, which covered the whole *ringhiera* of the Palagio de' Signoria, and then a scaffolding which began at the *ringhiera* next to the 'lion' and reached into the middle of the piazza, towards the Tetto dei Pisani; and here was erected a solid piece of wood many *braccia* high, and round this a large circular platform. On the aforesaid piece of wood was placed a horizontal one in the shape of a cross; but people noticing it said: 'They are going to crucify him'; and when these murmurs were heard, orders were given to saw off part of the wood, so that it should not look like a cross.[17]

Making a martyr out of these men was something that both the Signoria and the papal commissioners wanted to avoid at all costs. The removal of the wooden beam that made the scaffold look like a cross can only attest to that – it would do no good for the reputation of the Signoria if Savonarola could be later compared with Christ. What mattered now was seeing that the sentence was carried out as soon as possible, and a date was set for the following morning. Girolamo Savonarola, who had once taken Florence by storm, was about to go down in flames.

# Chapter 13

# Martyrdom

In his cell in the tower of the Piazza della Signoria, Savonarola would have known nothing about the fate that had been decided for him. The first indicator would have been when footsteps echoed on the stone steps outside his cell and the heavy wooden door opened, revealing a number of officials, including the one who had put him through so much pain early in his trials, Ser Ceccone. They gathered in his cell, where he had been busy praying, and told him that the following morning he would be executed for his crimes. Seemingly at peace with the idea of death, he did not even bother speaking to his visitors, not even to ask how they would kill him. All he did was go back to his prayers. Pescia and Maruffi acted very differently from their master when they found out that they were to die in a matter of hours. Pescia wrote a letter of farewell to the friars at Fiesole, where he was prior. The letter included instructions about what they were to do with all of Savonarola's writings, which he had in his cell: they were to bind them into a book and keep them in the monastery so that those who came after could still learn from him.

Maruffi, who had tried to escape San Marco during the siege and during his trial too, was overcome with complete and utter terror. This has to be the most human reaction of the three. He begged the officials to be allowed to state his case before the people of Florence in an effort to save his own skin. He desperately wanted mercy and believed that the people would give it to him. The officials, of course, refused.

Their final night was spent in the company of a member of the Compagni de' Neri. These were a group of black-robed men whose job was to comfort the condemned in the hours before they were put to death. However the brother assigned to spend time with Savonarola was a known Medici supporter named Jacopo Niccolini. He had been chosen specifically to see if he could get any final pieces of information out of the condemned friar. But despite his anti-Savonarolan sentiments, Niccolini seemed to have developed respect for the broken prior of San Marco and was impressed with just how strong he was being in his final hours. So empathetic was he that when Savonarola asked if he could help arrange one last meeting with his two colleagues in order to offer them words of comfort before they met their ends, he agreed.

They were reunited shortly after. All three were taken to a room within the palazzo accompanied by members of the Benedictine Order who had been appointed as their confessors for that final night. Each of them prayed for life eternal and declared that their faith was unwavering. Maruffi prayed that he would escape purgatory and ascend directly to heaven, while also praying for strength when he met his fate on the scaffold. Pescia made it clear that he never believed the reports that Savonarola had recanted. Savonarola, on the other hand, addressed his two colleagues directly – he is said to have chided them for their reactions to the situation and the fact they had no idea how they should face their deaths. He also made it clear that neither of them should speak out about the sentence and say it was unjust. Pescia and Maruffi then knelt before Savonarola and received a blessing, before going back to their cells where they spent their remaining hours in the company of the Compagni de' Neri and prepared themselves for death.

Savonarola returned to his cell with Niccolini. Exhausted, he lay down with his head in Niccolini's lap and slept soundly. It was as if he were completely at peace with what was coming, and had fully accepted that there was no way out of it – there would be no clemency from the Pope and no forgiveness from the people of Florence. When he woke at dawn, requesting a drink of water, he is said to have turned to Niccolini and gave what can only be described as a prophecy:

You know the things I have pre-announced here and how I predicted many tribulations for this city. Now I want to inform you of the time of its greatest tribulation. Know that it will take place when there will be a Pope named Clement.[1]

Giulio de' Medici acceded to the papal throne in 1523, as Pope Clement VII.

As the time of the execution loomed, the three friars were allowed to celebrate one last Mass together. Savonarola asked whether he would be allowed to hold the Host for this last service; permission for which was granted. He and the friars then celebrated Mass and prayed for forgiveness from the city of Florence and her people.

Then it was time. On 23 May 1498, the three were led from the palazzo and as they came down the main stairs, they were met by Dominican friars who had been ordered to strip them of their robes. Savonarola was allowed, briefly, to hold the habit that had for so long covered his body. He held it in his arms and spoke to it: 'O holy habit, how much did I desire you! God gave you to me, and until now I have kept you pure; and even now I would not leave you, but you are taken from me!'[2]

Those words showed a man who not only believed his own innocence but who lamented the loss of something that had been his whole life. In what had seemed like the blink of an eye he had gone from the top of the hierarchy in Florence, where he had believed wholeheartedly in making the city pure again and ridding it of tyranny, to facing his death. Unfortunately he had made mistakes along the way and made enemies of the wrong people. His hard line against much of what the citizens loved had turned them against him and his outspoken methods had put him in a direct war with the Pope. It was a battle that he could not win, and one that had finally come to a close.

Now, stripped of the robes that had marked them out as members of the Dominican brotherhood, the three men walked out into the piazza barefoot and dressed in their undershirts.

The piazza was packed full of people, crammed together in order to watch the infamous Fra Girolamo Savonarola meet his end. The stage was set – a macabre piece of theatre to show that those who went against the Pope and the Republic of Florence could easily be destroyed. The people who crowded about the hastily erected scaffold jostled to get a view of the disgraced friars as they made their way forwards; they were expecting a show. Little did they know they would get a show that they would never forget.

Savonarola, Pescia and Maruffi were met by three separate tribunals. Each of these had individual roles to perform before the friars could be executed. The first was led by a Dominican and former prior of San Marco, who was armed with a brief from Alexander granting him permission to degrade the friars before their deaths – this meant that they would be stripped of their roles within the Church, allowing them to be judged and executed by the state of Florence. They would then be expelled from their orders and the Church, and would be formally condemned to death. The last step in the process would see them climbing the scaffold and facing the hangman.

In his diaries, Landucci described the ordeal faced by the friars as they met each of these tribunals:

> The sacrifice of the three Frati was made. They took them out of the *Palagio* and brought them on to the *ringhiera* where were assembled the 'Eight' and the Collegi, the papal envoy, the General of the Dominicans, and many canons, priests and monks of divers orders, and the Bishop of the Pagagliotti who was deputed to degrade the three Frati; and here on the *ringhiera* the said ceremony was to be performed. They were robed in all their vestments, which were taken off one by one, with the appropriate words for the degradation, it being constantly affirmed that Fra Girolamo was a heretic and schismatic, and on this account condemned to be burnt; then their faces and hands were shaved, as is customary in this ceremony. When this was complete, they left the Frati in the hands of the 'Eight' who immediately made the decision that they should be hung and burnt; and they were led straight on to the platform at the foot of the cross.[3]

During the first stage of the degradation, as the bishop stripped Savonarola of his place in the Church, he refused to look him in the eye. Instead he muttered over the declaration that formally expelled him: 'I separate you from the Church militant and from the Church triumphant.'[4]

Savonarola argued this point, stating that he did not have the power to separate him from the Church triumphant. Such jurisdiction only lay with God.

Following this, the three were met by Remolino who presented them with a plenary indulgence – all of their sins were forgiven and thus, once the execution was over, they would be spared the punishment of purgatory. But why had Alexander given this brief for Remolino to read out? The move seems hypocritical; but could it be that he was feeling a sense of guilt and wanted to make sure that once the friar had suffered physically, he would be safe spiritually?

They were then led towards the cross, as described in the passage by Landucci, where they were met by the executioner. The crowds who were jostling to find a space to get the best view, called out that now was the time for him to perform a miracle. If he could save himself, they would believe that he had been falsely accused and many within the crowd must have been hoping for this to happen. They would be disappointed.

Savonarola was not the first to die. That 'honour' went to the terrified Silvestro Maruffi. He climbed the ladder that was leaning on to the scaffold and the executioner placed a noose about his neck. Mistakes were made here that would make his end particularly nasty. The noose was not tightened enough and the chain that hung about his waist was not heavy enough, so when the condemned man was shoved from the ladder, he hung there choking slowly to death. These 'mistakes' were of course intentional. There would be no entertainment should the three condemned friars die too quickly, and, after all, both the Florentine government and the Pope wanted to make an example of them. The second man to die was Domenico da Pescia who happily climbed up the ladder towards his martyrdom. The last was Savonarola, who had been forced to watch the torment of his fellow brothers. He climbed the ladder silently, not having given any final scaffold speech. Now, as the condemned hung there above the as-yet unlit wood beneath them, the executioner played a little game. He took hold of the rope and jerked it about, making Savonarola's body jump and dance. But then as he began descending the ladder in order to light the fire, a member of the crowd rushed forward and grabbed a lit torch, setting fire to the pyre while shouting: 'Now I can burn the man who wanted to burn me!'[5]

Could it be that this man was a sodomite who wanted revenge for the fact that Savonarola had encouraged death by burning for homosexuals? It certainly seems likely.

Once all three had been hanged and the fires lit, they were to suffer more humiliation, as Landucci recorded:

> When all three were hung, Fra Girolamo being in the middle, facing the *Palagio*, the scaffold was separated from the *ringhiera*, and a fire was made on the circular platform round the cross, upon which the gunpowder was put and set alight, so that the said fire burst out with a noise of rockets and cracking. In a few hours they were burnt, their legs and arms gradually dropping off; part of their bodies remaining hanging to the chains, a quantity of stones were thrown to make them fall, as there was a fear of the people getting hold of them.[6]

As the flames raged, the wind caught Savonarola's body and caused his arm to raise as if he were blessing the gathered citizens. They cried out that it was a miracle, that God was saving him, but were disappointed as the flames quickly covered his body. Landucci's account continued:

> And then the hangman and those whose business it was, hacked down the post and burnt it on the ground, bringing a lot of brushwood, and stirring the fire up over the dead bodies, so that the very least piece was consumed. Then they fetched carts and accompanied by the macebearers, carried the last bit of dust to the Arno, by the Ponte Vecchio, in order that no remains should be found.[7]

When the ashes were scooped up and dumped in the river, it showed Savonarola's followers that the friar was less than nothing and prevented any of them from getting their hands on his remains to keep as a relic. It was also aimed at neutralising all support for the friar, to show that he had not been the religious man and prophet that so many had believed him to be.

Despite this, his supporters still tried to find evidence of his innocence. As the trial records were printed and circulated, rumours started that the documents had been tampered with by Savonarola's torturer, Ser Ceccone. The rumours were true. It was whispered that Ceccone had admitted he had added false information into the transcript – such as the claims from Savonarola that he was a heretic – on the order of his superiors. Such talk would have given those who supported the friar some comfort in the dark days following his arrest and execution.

But, of course, those who stood against the friar and his supporters also had their say following the execution, and they continued to blacken his name. Historian Donald Weinstein describes how his enemies resorted to a supernatural explanation for Savonarola's activities:

> In an exculpatory letter to the College of Cardinals written soon after the Frate's execution, Marsilio Ficino explained that it was no ordinary human hypocrite who had deceived the Florentines but an astute demon, servant of malicious astral forces – Antichrist himself. Audaciously simulating virtue and hiding his vices, mixing his prophecies with lies, he had, Ficino said, convinced the crowd of the truth of his predictions until even he himself believed in them … . For all its paranoia and craven bombast, Ficino's reading of Savonarola's career was psychologically perceptive on a key point which neither the crestfallen Piagnoni nor triumphant Arabbiati seem to have grasped – that the great preacher may have deceived no one more than himself.[8]

Girolamo Savonarola was gone. His enemies finally had their wish in making the troublesome friar disappear. But as his ashes floated down the Arno, and his enemies continued to blacken his reputation, his name lived on, much to the detriment of his enemies. Days after his execution, a number of women were found kneeling and praying at the spot in which he had burned. Decades after his death, his teachings were being used during the Protestant Reformation. And yet many still believed him to be a fraud. Just as he had divided Florence during his life, he continued to divide both Florence and the Catholic Church years after his death.

# Chapter 14

# Legacy

With Savonarola dead, Florence was free to slip back into a life of vice. Everything that he had worked for dissolved within mere moments and vice once more reigned supreme. Sodomy, gambling and whoring were once more the order of the day. Landucci notes:

> Everyone had been indulging in a vicious life, and at night-time one saw halberds or naked swords all over the city, and men gambling by candlelight in the Mercato Nuovo and everywhere without shame. Hell seemed open; and woe to him who should try to reprove vice.[1]

But just a few years after his death, Savonarola's supporters once more came to the fore when French forces commanded by Louis XII returned to Italy. The New Cyrus who had been promised in Charles VIII had been reborn in Louis, and as such many of Savonarola's supporters believed that his prophecy was finally coming true. Savonarola's works once more poured from Florentine printers and support for the late Friar once more became fashionable in the city. In 1500 Louis took Milan and imprisoned Ludovico Sforza, who told some Florentine merchants to pass on the message that Savonarola was indeed a true prophet. There were many who also wished to canonise Savonarola, but this never happened as Pope Julius II was incensed with the Florentines for allowing a council to take place in the city, a council that had it been successful, would have led to his deposition. Perhaps had they not called this council; Savonarola would have become a saint. Such a thing would have been tantamount to spitting in the face of his enemies.

Even until 1527, when Charles V sacked Rome, people were still believing that Girolamo Savonarola's influence was paramount, and his prophecies were coming true. Charles V in this instance would take the place of both Charles VIII and Louis XII as the scourge from beyond the Alps, a scourge that would overthrow the papacy once and for all. Again, many voiced their opinion that Savonarola had been a true prophet, a saint and a man of God. And for a while, Florence once more became a true Republic. With the Medici gone, the support of Savonarola's *piagnoni* came to the fore despite the friar being long dead, they made to rebuild his City of God. Once again laws were passed banning gambling and sodomy, blasphemers and sodomites were put to death while the processions begun in Savonarola's day now happened daily. It was not to last. Following a long, drawn out siege, Florence once more gave itself over to Medici rule. The family returned in triumph in the August of 1530 after once again having been exiled from the city. Ippolito de Medici and his brother Alessandro had been forced to flee the city after a popular uprising in 1527 three years later and prospects for the city had changed. Ippolito was now a cardinal and had no prospect of ruling. Alessandro, the bastard son of Lorenzo de Medici and a slave, would become Duke of Florence and on 5 July 1531, he entered Florence as its Duke, and would once more revive the tyranny that Savonarola had so detested.

With the Medici back in Florence, they would have been highly aware that there were still those who supported Savonarola's ideals. The city was still divided over the friar, yet when it was suggested once more than Savonarola be canonised in the late 1590s, the Medici blocked the idea. Prayers were said for the friar until 1634 when the Vatican finally forbade such actions. Flowers were also placed on the spot where Savonarola was executed each 23 May, Savonarola's feast day, until 1770. The tradition has recently been renewed and every 23 May, the people of Florence commemorate Savonarola's memory by placing flowers upon the plaque that marks the place of his death.[2]

Savonarola has long divided historians and now, with the introduction of his character into modern historical television adaptations, many see him simply as a fanatic who burned priceless works of art and fought against the Catholic Church. In recent years he has been seen in both *The Borgias* and *Borgia: Faith and Fear*. Both series show him as a religious fanatic who burned for his crimes against the Pope.

A character as dramatic and multi-layered as Savonarola was bound to attract artists, playwrights, novelists and film-makers long after his death. In 1884, the Irish composer Charles Stanford produced an opera based on his life which was first performed in Hamburg. A number of German writers found him fascinating, but the only British great who made him her hero was George Eliot, in her novel *Remola* in 1863, at a time when all things Italian was front-page news because of the recent re-unification of the country. In that context, the liberator Giuseppe Garibaldi drew thousands of supporters at various lectures throughout Britain.

On the big screen, the friar missed out. *Prince of Foxes* (1949), starring Hollywood heart-throb Tyrone Power with a compelling Orson Welles as Cesare Borgia, is set two years after the man's death. Charlton Heston's *The Agony and the Ecstasy* (1961), based on the novel by Irving Stone, deals with Florence and the Medici but not Savonarola.

On television, the first *Borgias* series in 1981 focused on Cesare and Lucrezia Borgia and Pope Alexander VI, but, again, no mention of the friar. It was the second outing of that extraordinary family, between 2011 and 2013 that introduced the character to a new generation. Played by a suitably Machiavellian Steven Berkoff, the complexities of the man were lost in the over-simplification perhaps necessary for modern television audiences. In the event, the series was cancelled early because of prohibitive costs, a problem which the producer of *Prince of Foxes* had encountered over sixty years before.

As technology has changed, historical characters assume a life of their own to suit the needs of an audience. The phenomenally successful *Assassins Creed* video game, produced by Ubisoft in 2007 was followed two years later by a sequel in which Savonarola is the central target of the assassins.

The problem with all this appropriation of Savonarola is that reality fades and he becomes, ultimately, a computer-generated nothing that goes through predictable motions to appeal to a generation that has little grasp of history and cannot tell real characters from fictional ones. Perhaps a wider and in some ways more disturbing issue is that there is a tendency to hijack a figure from the past and give them twenty-first century attitudes and outlooks. This happened historically (see below) but it is most obvious in the realms of fiction. The various paintings and statues of Savonarola portray a demented spirit, eyes staring, fingers spread like talons, a friar's hood menacingly over his face. Even a recent, supposedly serious, article in the *Guardian* has an opening sentence denouncing Savonarola as an ugly, violent man. In that sense, he fits perfectly into the role of television baddie and video game monster and we have lost sight of the real man and his times in all that.[3]

But Savonarola was so much more than a man who achieved great things for Florence within the few years that he held centre stage. And as religious men in the future would notice, specifically Martin Luther, Girolamo Savonarola was well aware of the vices that corrupted the Catholic Church. Savonarola tried his best to begin a rebuilding of the church, a road that Martin Luther would follow.

There are those who see Girolamo Savonarola as a precursor of the Reformation. By the early sixteenth century, the corruption and moral decay of the Catholic Church was all too obvious. John Wycliffe, Jan Hus, Girolamo Savonarola had all gone before, each with a different philosophy but having the common ground that the enemy was the church of Rome. It was the Dominican monk Martin Luther who brought an increasing tension to Europe to a head.

Born on 10 November 1483 in the small town of Eisleben to Hans Luther and his wife Margarethe, he spent his childhood in the city of Mansfeld. As the boy grew, surrounded by a number of siblings, his father wanted him to study law and he was sent to a number of top schools before attending the University of Erfurt. After graduating, he enrolled in law school but dropped out straight away. It was not for him and, in his mind, law was far too uncertain a subject. He wanted to study philosophy and religion, eventually deciding that religion was far more important than philosophy. And so in 1505 he made the decision to enter into monastic life. It was certainly not a popular choice with his parents. When he wrote to them asking for their approval, his father absolutely refused to give it.

After ordination in 1507, Luther found himself studying once again, but this time at the university of Wittenberg. He received a doctorate in theology five years later. From then on, after a shaky start when he doubted whether he had made the right career choice, his success went from strength to strength.

As a thinking man, however, Luther became disturbed over the issue of the sale of indulgences. It was possible to buy one's way into the Kingdom of Heaven and to avoid purgatory with old-fashioned cash. This was the role of the pardoner in Chaucers *Canterbury Tales* and any number of popes had granted absolution to men embarking on crusade because the murder of infidels did not count as a sin. The cost here was taking the cross and putting one's life on the line in the first place. So Luther wrote the *Disputation of Martin Luther on the Power and Efficacy of Indulgences* and pinned his 95 theses to the door of Wittenberg cathedral. This was, according to legend, on 31 October 1517, the eve of All Saints Day, which later would morph into the decidedly anti-Christian Halloween.

The printing press was already in use across Europe (the best selling books of the time were the Bible and the lurid, blood-thirsty account of Vlad Tepes, the Impaler, who had ruled Wallachia (today's Romania) until his death in battle in 1476. Even so, printed books were expensive and Luther wanted to advertise the Church's corruption quickly and cheaply. By law, everyone in Wittenberg attended the cathedral and the impact was immediate and intense.

Condemned by his local bishop and the leading secular powers of the area, Luther refused to apologise or recant and risked excommunication, exile and even death. Eventually, by 1520, the world had changed. 'Here I stand, said Luther, I can do no other.' His exile and excommunication stood, but he got away with his life and lived unhappily ever after, tormented by guilt at having done more than his bit to destroy the church that had raised him.

As with Jan Hus, so with Martin Luther. So with Girolamo Savonarola. Others used their theological and moral disputes to strengthen their own power and to weaken the Church. After centuries of paying extortionate taxation to Rome, the peasants in various parts of what would become Germany went on the rampage, attacking priests and burning churches. Outraged at their irreverent behaviour, the gentry and nobility retaliated, burning villages and slaughtering peasants. The Peasants' War and the Knights' War of the 1520s set the scene on over a century of internecine warfare across Europe, fought in the name of religion.

Martin Luther had not intended any of this, any more than Hus and Savonarola had. It was their followers who twisted things for their own ends. There is no doubt that the man took the Florentine friar as a role model. He wrote an introduction to Savonarola's works, especially the meditations from prison and recommended his texts to others. But Luther went much further than Savonarola had. While the Florentine focused on the virtues of the scriptures and the corruption of the Church, Luther believed in *solo fide* (by faith alone). To reach Heaven, all a man needs is a belief in God; the priesthood is merely in the way. Man speaks to God; God speaks to man. Where is the priest in all that? Thousands of peasants all over Europe took Martin Luther at his word.

It was the second generation of reformers however which provides the best parallel with Savonarola. In response to Luther, the Catholic Church fought back. First, it produced the *Index Prohibitorum*, a list of anti-Catholic books which good Christians were not allowed to own, or even to read. Ironically, bearing in mind the bonfire of the vanities, Savonarola's works were included. In town squares all over Europe, bonfires of heretical texts roared into the night sky. Centuries later, the German poet Heinrich Heine wrote that a society that burns books today will burn people tomorrow and so it happened with the Catholic Church. The Council of Trent in 1543, like Constance thirty years earlier, laid down the harsh ground-rules of a church that was entrenched in its position, fighting for survival. The Holy Inquisition had been set up centuries earlier by Pope Innocent III to combat the Albigensian heresy of the early thirteenth century. Now it was given sweeping new powers, creating the ghastly spectacle of the *auto da fe* (act of faith) in which supposed heretics were burned alive at the stake, with or without the mercy of being garrotted with wire first. It was out of their religious hysteria that the witch craze of the sixteenth and seventeenth centuries was born. The third enactment of the Counter-Reformation was the creation of the Society of Jesus in 1540 by a Spanish ex-soldier, Ignatius Loyola. The positive side of this was that the Society offered simple rules which (by now confused) Catholics could follow to lead good Christian lives. The flip-side was that the Jesuits became a feared organization in their own right, associated with militant fanaticism and they were outlawed by a number of European states in the years ahead.

By the middle of the sixteenth century, the Old World was a religious battleground. And some of this spilled over into the New World too. France remained staunchly Catholic with a Huguenot (Protestant) minority. Italy and Spain were faithful to the papacy too, but Germany was split between the old faith and the new, leading to religious wars still being fought a century later. Northern Europe by contrast was Protestant, but Catholic enclaves remained everywhere.

The figure who emerged amidst all this chaos and in many ways the most like Savonarola was Jehan Cauvin, known to history as John Calvin. He was born in Picardy, France, in 1509 and, like many in this book, was destined for a career in the Church. He was even given a tonsure (a monk's haircut) at the age of twelve as a symbol of his leanings. Unlike Savonarola, however, Calvin became absorbed in the Humanist leaning of his day and studied law first at Orleans University, then at Bourges.

He experienced a religious conversion sometime around 1530 and it was this perhaps that has marked him out, in our secular age, as an eccentric or even mentally disturbed. In eighteenth century England, John Wesley had a similar experience 'I felt I *did* trust in God, in God alone, for my salvation' while attending an Anglican service in London. With his penchant for open-air preaching and his concern for the poor of England's burgeoning working class, Wesley's detractors wrote him off as mad. For Calvin, too, this has been a conclusion for some writers, especially in relation to his work in Geneva.

Europe's universities were riven in the 1530s and 40s, not only by the rise of Lutheranism but by the same debates between Humanists and the more conservative elements of the Catholic Church that had occupied Savonarola. Calvin was in the centre of all this, but he had as his background the growing literature of the Reformation and the ground-breaking work of men like Luther, Melanchthon and Zwingli.

It was in Basel in 1536 that Calvin published his first and greatest work, *Institutes of Christian Religion*. Which he was on his way to Strasbourg when he stayed overnight in the Swiss town of Geneva. The one-night stay turned into something far longer and Geneva became the headquarters of Calvinism with its precepts of the elect, the chosen few on whom God has smiled and an unshakeable belief in predestination. It is difficult for us to find a doctrine that is more divisive. Used as we are to equality, of faiths, political slants and gender, the concept of a pre-selected elite which cannot be changed is grimly depressing. It is euphoric if one believes that one is elite, but anyone outside the hallowed circle is condemned to a life of misery and one without the certainty of Heaven.

Geneva itself was a decidedly backward town, surrounded by far more forward-thinking areas happy to abandon the Catholic Church and move on. Just as Savonarola found himself clashing with the Medici and the council in Florence, so Calvin was at odds with the conservative council of Geneva and he was opposed by wealthy, titled families. For the best part of fifteen years, a vicious war was raged between Calvin's followers and the council whom he called libertines because they rejected the harsh religious code that he laid down.

Perhaps more than any single member of the Reformation, John Calvin can be seen as the instigator of Puritanism. Today, when secular values rule and nearly every church has a shrinking congregation, Puritanism in all its forms is unpopular. It was at best silly, counter to man's basic humanity and at worst it was a fatally harsh regime that killed people. In seventeenth-century England, for example, lunatic sects grew up, like the Fifth Monarchy Men, whose families laid an extra place at their tables for Christ, in case he should turn up at their homes for the Third Coming. Others, unhappy with an increasingly rigid Puritan regime at home, set sail on board the *Mayflower* to found even more extreme communities in America.

Virtually everything laid down by law under Oliver Cromwell and his Major-Generals in the England of the 1650s was already established in Geneva by Calvin a century earlier. All elements of the Catholic Church were dismissed as superstition, a move that would culminate in England in the iconoclasm of Henry VIII's dissolution of the monasteries and the soldiers of the New Model Army under Cromwell. Sexual morality was closely monitored. Calvin himself was happily married and he expected everyone to follow Biblical precepts in that respect. Adultery, prostitution and sodomy were punishable by death. Taverns were carefully regulated and drunkenness prohibited. Dancing was the work of the devil; it culminated, forty years later, at Salem, Massachusetts in accusations of witchcraft against wholly innocent people. Gambling in Geneva was illegal, the relatively new pack of cards was the devil's picture book. Even swearing was outlawed; in the next century, a blaspheming trooper in Cromwell's New Model Army could expect to have an iron spike driven through his tongue.

And in Geneva, Calvin burned people. His opponents, members of the council, even Protestant leaners with a different take on religion, would find themselves with their heads shaved and their feet in the faggots because they failed to live up to Calvin's ideals.

It is one of the ironies of history that while John Calvin behaved just as badly in Geneva as Savonarola did in Florence, the world has been far kinder to the Frenchman than to the Italian. Perhaps because Calvin had a dogma and a vision that extended far beyond an attack on the papacy and the corruption of the Church, people followed him beyond the walls of Geneva and he has become an international figure of repute.

Under Savonarola's rule, Florence almost became the Godly City that he so desperately wanted. He reformed the church within the city and aimed to reform it within the higher echelons of Church society. Sadly for Savonarola, his methods ended up being far too like the tyranny of the Medici and attracted the attention of those who could, and did, bring about his downfall.

Savonarola's life came to an end in the most horrendous of ways. Tortured to confession, he was then hanged and burned, and his ashes thrown unceremoniously into the river Arno. Yet despite Pope Alexander VI's insistence that Savonarola's reputation be completely tarnished, despite his insistence that nothing remained of the friar's body, Girolamo Savonarola still became a martyr and he has remained a hero to the Dominicans with whom he had lived and worked for so many years.

Like all great figures of the past, Savonarola has been hijacked by later generations and moulded into their own image. When the loose confederation of states that made up Italy determined on unification the *Risorgimento* in 1859, the friar's name was invoked as a champion of the people. This notion, that somehow Savonarola was a democrat is laughably wrong, but it is typical of modern political groups. In 1919, a Communist organization in Germany called itself the Spartacus League after the gladiator slave who took on the Roman empire in the first century BC. Spartacus was no more a champion of the working man than Savonarola was, but that does not stop the ill-informed stealing the name. In that same year, an Italian group calling itself the Peoples Party took Savonarola's name for its propaganda purposes. Italy had been on the winning side in the First World War but had precious little to show for it and Europe generally was about to be convulsed by a war for men's minds every bit as all-consuming as the Reformation; the clash between Communism and Fascism. In that struggle, Savonarola and the Peoples Party were eclipsed by Benito Mussolini and his Fascisti.

Yet, despite Pope Alexander VI's insistence that Savonarola's reputation be completely tarnished, despite his insistence that nothing remained of the friar's body, Girolamo Savonarola still became a martyr and he has remained a hero to the Dominicans with whom he lived and worked for so many years.

We do not know if the Florentine friar had a sense of humour or a sense of irony; such things are rarely recorded about anybody in the past. But if he did, I wonder what he would have made of the fact that today's Catholic Church is considering making him a saint?

# Notes

**Chapter 1**
1. Trans. Linda Villari, Pasquale Villari, *Life and Times of Girolamo Savonarola* (T. Fisher Unwin 1888) p. 13
2. Plinio Prioreschi, *A History of Medicine: Medieval Medicine* (Horatius Press 1996) p. 657
3. 'Venuto all'eta d' imparare costume e lettere, fece vivente acora l' avolo fuo, non mediocre progresso nella grammtica & nella latiná', Pacifico Burlamacchi, *Vita del P. F. Girolamo Savonarola*, (Nella Stamperia di Jacopo Giusti, 1764) p. 4
4. Desmond Seward, *The Burning of the Vanities: Savonarola and the Borgia Pope* (Sutton 2006) p. 8; Donald Weinstein, *Savonarola: The Rise and Fall of a Renaissance Prophet* (Yale 2011) p. 8
5. Weinstein 2011 p. 10
6. Burlamacchi 1764 p. 5
7. Weinstein 2011 p. 11
8. Girolamo Savonarola, *Sermon: Predica XIX sopra Aggeo* (delivered on 19 December 1494)
9. Paul Strathern, *Death in Florence* (Jonathan Cape 2011) p. 46
10. Lauro Martines, *Scourge and Fire: Savonarola and Renaissance Italy* (Pimlico 2007) p. 14

**Chapter 2**
1. Burlamacchi 1764 p. 5
2. Weinstein 2011 p. 20
3. Elizabeth Lev, *The Countess of Forli: Renaissance Italy's Most Courageous and Notorious Countess Caterina Riario Sforza de' Medici* (Houghton Mifflin Harcourt 2011) p. 26
4. Christopher Hibbert, *The Rise and Fall of The House Of Medici* (Penguin 1979) p. 131
5. Miles J. Unger, *Magnifico: The Brilliant Life and Violent Times of Lorenzo de' Medici* (Simon & Schuster 2009) p. 302
6. Lauro Martines, *April Blood: Florence and the Plot against the Medici* (Pimlico 2004) p. 116
7. Paul Strathern, *The Medici: Godfathers of the Renaissance* (Vintage 2007) p. 163
8. Martines pp. 116–118; Hibbert 1979 p. 138
9. Eventually a myth grew up surrounding the murder that it was committed on Easter Sunday. This was carried on by the Medici family who wanted to slur the Pazzi name as much as possible.

10. Hibbert 1979 p. 136
11. Seward 2006 p. 38
12. Christopher Hibbert, *Florence: The Biography of a City* (Penguin 1994) pp. 350–1
13. Hibbert 1979 p. 179

### Chapter 3

1. Trans. Cecil Grayson, Roberto Ridolfi, *The Life of Girolamo Savonarola* (Routledge 1959) p. 23
2. *Ibid* pp. 24
3. Burlamacchi 1764 pp. 15–16; Weinstein 2011 p. 67; Strathern 2011 p. 96
4. Michael Mallet & Christine Shaw, *The Italian Wars: 1494–1559* (Routledge 2014) p. 105
5. Strathern 2011 p. 51; Weinstein 2011 p. 27
6. Villari 1888 p. 74
7. Trans. Sir Thomas More, Giovanni F. Pico, *Giovanni Pico della Mirandola: His life by his nephew Giovanni Francesco Pico, also three of his letters, his interpretations of Psalm XVI; his twelve rules of a Christian and his Deprecatory hymn to God,* (Benediction Classics Oxford 2008) p. 8
8. Strathern 2011 p. 52
9. Villari 1888 p. 75
10. Farmer, S. A., *Syncretism in the West: Pico's 900 Theses 1486* (Medieval & Renaissance Text & Studies 1998) p. 3
11. Seward 2006 p. 28
12. Pico 2008 p. 11
13. V. Romano (ed), Girolamo Savonarola, *Prediche sopra Ruth e Michea* Vol II (Belardetti Rome 1962) p. 91
14. Trans. Anne Borelli & Maria P. Passaro, *Selected Writings of Girolamo Savonarola: Religion and Politics, 1490–1498* (Yale University Press 2006) p. 59
15. Ridolfi 1959 p. 33
16. Seward 2006 p. 59
17. Unger 2009 p. 424
18. Strathern 2011 p. 107
19. *Ibid* p. 108
20. Janet Ross, *Lives of the Early Medici: As Told in their Correspondence* (Chatto & Windus 1910) p. 332
21. Ridolfi 1959 p. 49
22. This refers to Lorenzo's taking of public funds meant for the dowries of young women in the city, as well as taking money belonging to younger members of the Medici family.
23. Unger 2009 p. 436

### Chapter 4

1. Unger 2009 p. 37
2. Dale Kent, *Cosimo de' Medici and the Florentine Renaissance* (Yale University Press 2000) p. 319
3. Hibbert 1979 p. 113
4. Strathern 2007 p. 152

5. Quoted in Unger 2009 pp. 172–73
6. *Ibid* p. 187

## Chapter 5

1. Johannes Nesius (Giovanni Nesi), *Oraculum de Novo Saeculo* (Lorenzo de' Morgiani 1497) p. 23
2. Christopher S. Calenza, *Piety and Pythagoras in Renaissance Florence: The Symbolum Nesianum* (Brill 2001) p. 41
3. *Ibid* p. 45
4. Strathern 2011 pp. 230–231
5. Trans. Sidney Alexander, Francesco Guicciardini, *The History of Italy* (Princeton University Press 1984) p. 122
6. Charles Trinkaus (ed), with Heiko A. Overman, *The Pursuit of Holiness: Volume X* (E. J. Brill 1974) p. 252
7. Alessio Assontis, *Fra Girolamo Savonarola and the aesthetics of pollution in fifteenth-century Rome* in Mark Bradley (ed), with Kenneth Stow, *Rome, Pollution and Propriety: Dirt, Disease and Hygiene in the Eternal City from Antiquity to Modernity* (Cambridge University Press 2012) p. 143
8. Seward 2006 p. 122
9. Martines 2007 p. 77
10. Strathern 2011 p. 233
11. Guicciardini 1984 p. 85
12. Martines 2007 pp. 78–79
13. *Ibid* p. 81
14. *Ibid* p. 90

## Chapter 6

1. Quoted in Unger 2008 p. 222
2. *Ibid* p. 366
3. Strathern 2007 p. 207
4. Ridolfi 1959 p. 56
5. Mallet & Shaw 2014 p. 144
6. E. L. S. Horsburgh, *Girolamo Savonarola* (Knight & Millet 1901) pp. 98–99
7. Seward 2006 p. 79
8. Seward 2006 p. 85; Weinstein 2011 p. 143; Pico 2008 p. 23
9. Weinstein 2011 p. 143; Girolamo Savonarola, *Prediche sopra aggeo 104* (23 November 1494)
10. Strathern 2007 p. 213
11. Martines 2007 p. 42
12. *Ibid* p. 61; Weinstein 2011 p. 80

## Chapter 7

1. Cited in Paul Strathern, *The Borgias: Power and Fortune* (Atlantic 2019) p. 35
2. Trans. Gilda Roberts, Ivan Cloudes, *The Borgias* (New York 1989) p. 33
3. G. J. Meyer, *The Borgias: The Hidden History* (New York 2013) pp. 101; Orestres Ferrara, *The Borgia Pope* (London 1942) p. 56
4. Strathern 2019 p. 56

5. *Ibid*
6. Trans Lodovico Domenichi, Paolo Giovio, *Delle Istorie Del Suo Tempo: Prima Parte* (Rocca 1565) p. 121
7. Steffano Infessura, *Diario della Citta di Roma* (Roma 1890) p. 282
8. Ferrara 1942 p. 125

### Chapter 8
1. Ferrara 1942 p. 236
2. Strathern 2011 p. 240
3. *Ibid* pp. 240-241
4. Seward 2006 p. 130
5. Quoted in Hibbert 1979 p. 196; Strathern 2011 p. 255; Seward 2006 p. 158
6. Horsburgh 1901 p. 147
7. Girolamo Savonarola, *Triumph of the Cross* (Sands & Co, 1901) pp. 42-43
8. *Ibid*
9. Seward 2006 pp. 222-224
10. *Ibid* pp. 229-232

### Chapter 9
1. Seward 2006 p. 162
2. Strathern 2011 p. 258
3. Trans. Alice de Rosen Jervis, Luca Landucci, *A Florentine Diary from 1450 to 1516* (J. M. Dent & Sons 1927) pp. 116-117
4. Jacob Burckhardt, *The Civilization of the Renaissance in Italy* (Phaidon Press 1995) p. 314
5. Seward 2006 p. 219
6. *Ibid* p. 176
7. Hibbert 1994 p. 157
8. Seward p. 220

### Chapter 10
1. Weinstein 2011 p. 228
2. *Ibid* p. 229
3. Ridolfi 1959 pp. 198-199
4. Martines 2007 p. 169
5. *Ibid* p. 173
6. *Et cosi miserabile spetaculo fini aore otto, nel quale punti il magistrato dette l'ultimo colpo in su la manaia, et taglio il capo a Bernardo del Nero, che guen' aveva data quatro et taglo tutto il mento.* In Joseph Schnitzer & Bartolomeo Cerretani, *Quellen und Forshungen zur Gershichte Savonarolas* (Verlag der J. J. Lenter'schen Buchhandlung 1904) p. 51
7. Quoted in Seward 2006 p. 195
8. *Ibid* p. 200
9. *Ibid* p. 203
10. Quoted in Seward 2006, p. 229; Villari 1888, pp. 644-645
11. Strathern 2011 p. 305
12. *Ibid* p. 308

**Chapter 11**
1. Quoted in Strathern 2011 p. 317
2. Landucci 1927 p. 136
3. *Ibid* pp. 136-137
4. Strathern 2011 p. 324
5. Landucci 1927 p. 137
6. *Ibid* p. 138
7. Seward 2006 p. 243
8. *Ibid*
9. *Ibid* p. 246

**Chapter 12**
1. Hibbert 1994 p. 325
2. Landucci 1927 p. 138
3. Villari 1888 p. 700
4. Quoted in Strathern 2011 p. 334
5. Quoted in Seward 2011 p. 280
6. Landucci 1927 p. 139
7. John K. Brackett, *Criminal Justice and Crime in Late Renaissance Florence 1537–1609* (Cambridge University Press 2002) p. 62
8. Quoted in Seward 2006 p. 252
9. Villari 1888 p. 721
10. *Ibid* p. 724
11. *Ibid* p. 744
12. Strathern 2011 p. 354
13. *Ibid* pp. 354-355
14. Seward 2006 p. 260
15. *Ibid*
16. *Ibid* p. 261
17. Landucci 1927 p. 142

**Chapter 13**
1. Quoted in Weinstein 2011 p. 294
2. Quoted in Ridolfi 1959 p. 269
3. Landucci 1927 pp. 142-143
4. Quoted in Strathern 2011 p. 363
5. Seward 2006 p. 267
6. Landucci 1927 p. 143
7. *Ibid*
8. Weinstein 2011 p. 297

**Chapter 14**
1. Landucci 1927 p. 145
2. Catherine Fletcher, *The Black Prince of Florence: The Spectacular Life and Treacherous World of Alessandro de' Medici* (The Bodley Head 2016) p. 77
3. Tamar Herzig, *Savonarola's Women: Visions and Reform in Renaissance Italy* (University of Chicago Press 2007) p. 4

# Bibliography and Further Reading

Alexander, Sidney (trans.); Guicciardini, Francesco, *The History of Italy*, Princeton University Press 1969

Anonymous, *Hyeronimo Savonarola: Historia breve della vita e delle predicazioni del frate domenicano*, Cirelli & Zanirato 2006

Behringer, George, F. (trans.); Rein, William, *The Life of Martin Luther*, Funk & Wagnalls 1883

Betz, Timothy, *The Artist and the Friar: Botticelli and the Business of Art – A Thesis in Art History*, Unpublished: Pennsylvania State University 2006

Borelli, Anne & Passaro Maria, P. (trans.), *Selected Writings of Girolamo Savonarola: Religion and Politics 1490–1498*, Yale University Press 2006

Burckhardt, Jacob, *The Civilization of the Renaissance in Italy*, Phaidon 1995

Burlamacchi, Pacifico, *Vita del P. F. Girolamo Savonarola del O. D. PR*, Nella Stamperia di Jacopo Giusti 1764

Cerretani, Bartolomeo & Schnitzer, Joseph, *Quellen und Forsehungen zur Geschicte Savonarolas*, Munchen J. J. Lenter 1902

Donnelly, John, P (trans.); Savonarola, Girolamo, *Prison Meditations on Psalms 51 & 31*, Marquette University Press 2011

Ferrara, Orestes, *The Borgia Pope*, Sheed & Ward 1942

Grayson, Cecil (trans.); Ridolfi, Roberto, *The Life of Girolamo Savonarola*, Routledge 1959

Hibbert, Christopher, *Florence: The Bibliography of a City*, Penguin 1994

Hibbert, Christopher, *The Rise and Fall of the House of Medici*, Penguin 1979

Horsburgh, E. L. S., *Girolamo Savonarola*, Knight & Millet 1901

Jervis, Alice de R. (trans.); Landucci Luca, *A Florentine Diary*, J.M. Dent & Sons 1927

Kent, Dale, *Cosimo de' Medici and the Florentine Renaissance*, Yale University Press 2006

Lev, Elizabeth, *The Tigress of Forli: Renaissance Italy's Most Courageous and Notorious Countess – Caterina Riario Sforza de' Medici*, Houghton Mifflin 2011

Mallet, Michael E. and Shaw, Christine, *The Italian Wars 1494–1559*, Routledge 2014

Martines, Lauro, *Scourge and Fire: Savonarola and Renaissance Italy*, Pimlico 2007

More, Thomas (trans.); Pico della Mirandola, Giovanni, F., *Giovanni Pico della Mirandola: His life by his nephew Giovanni Francesco Pico, also three of his letters, his interpretations of Psalm XVI; his Twelve rules of a Christian and his Deprecatory hymn to God*, Benediction Classics 2008

Morris, Samantha, *Girolamo Savonarola: The Renaissance Preacher*, MadeGlobal 2017

Nesi, Giovanni, *Oraculum de novo Saeculo*, Lorenzo de' Morgiani 1497

Olin, John C., *The Catholic Reformation: Savonarola to Ignatius Loyola*, Fordham University Press 1992

Pico della Mirandola, Giovanni, *Vita di Hieronimo Savonarola*, Sismel 1998

Prioreschi, Plinio, *A History of Medicine: Medieval Medicine*, Horatius Press 1996

Rosito, Massimiliano G., *Savonarola: Revisitato (1498–1998)*, Cita di Vita 1998

Savonarola, Girolamo, *The Triumph of the Cross*, Sands & Co 1901

Seward, Desmond, *The Burning of the Vanities: Savonarola and the Borgia Pope*, Sutton 2006

Strathern, Paul, *Death in Florence: The Medici, Savonarola and the Battle for the Soul of the Renaissance City*, Jonathan Cape 2011

Strathern, Paul, *The Medici: Godfather's of the Renaissance*, Vintage 2007

Unger, Miles J. *Magnifico: The Brilliant Life and Violent Times of Lorenzo de' Medici*, Simon & Schuster 2008

Villari, Linda (trans.); Villari, Pasquale, *Life and Times of Girolamo Savonarola*, T. Fisher Unwin 1888

Weinstein, Donald, *Savonarola and Florence: Prophecy and Patriotism in the Renaissance*, Princeton University Press 1970

Weinstein, Donald, *Savonarola: The Rise and Fall of a Renaissance Prophet*, Yale 2011

Worsley, Henry, *The Life of Martin Luther: Vol. I*, Bell and Daldy 1856

# Index